ARKANSIPPI MEMWARS

Books By Eugene B. Redmond

Poetry
Blues-Ode to the Fore-Dreamers
The Eye in the Ceiling
In A Time of Rain & Desire
Consider Loneliness as These Things
Songs from an Afro/Phone
River of Bones and Flesh and Blood
Sentry of the Four Golden Pillars

Poetry Pamphlets
A Tale of Time and Toilet Tissue
A Tale of Two Toms

Non-Fiction
Drumvoices: The Mission of Afro-American Poetry (A Critical History)

Anthologies
'Griefs of Joy': Contemporary Afro-American Poetry for Students
Sides of the River: A Mini-Anthology of Black Writings

Journals (Editor)
Black American Literature Forum, 1988 (Special Issue on Henry Dumas)
American Negro Literature Forum, 1972 (Special Black Poetry Issue)
Drumvoices: A Confluence of Literary, Cultural & Vision Arts (annual)
Break Word with the World (annual)

As Literary Executor of the Henry Dumas Estate
Echo Tree: Selected Fiction
Goodbye, Sweetwater: Selected Fiction
Knees of a Natural Man: Poetry
Rope of Wind and Other Stories
Jonoah and the Green Stone (novel)
Ark of Bones and Other Stories
Play Ebony Play Ivory (poems)
Poetry for My People

To Elzabeth Zelman —
Thanks for joining the Soular System 4
"Strength" to your writing hand.
Brotherly)
Eugene B. Redmond
10/3/2015

ARKANSIPPI
MEMWARS
Poetry, Prose & Chants
1962–2012

Eugene B. Redmond

TWP
THIRD WORLD PRESS
Progressive Publishing Since 1967

Chicago

Third World Press
Publishers since 1967
Chicago

First Edition
Printed in the United States of America

Library of Congress Cataloging-in-Publication
ISBN 13: 978-0-88378-347-4
Redmond, Eugene B., 1937

87654321

Works included in this book have appeared previously in *Aim, Blues-Ode to the Fore-Dreamers, Eighty Moods of Maya, The Eye in the Ceiling, fishwrap, In A Time of Rain & Desire, Kaiso! Writings by and about Katherine Dunham, Consider Loneliness as These Things, Songs from an Afro/Phone, River of Bones and Flesh and Blood, Sentry of the Four Golden Pillars, 'Griefs of Joy': Contemporary Afro-American Poetry for Students, Sides of the River: A Mini-Anthology of Black Writings, Black American Literature Forum*, 1988 (Special Double Issue on Henry Dumas), *American Negro Literature Forum*, 1972 (Special Black Poetry Issue), *Drumvoices: A Confluence of Literary, Cultural & Vision Arts* (annual since 1992), *Break Word with the World* (annual), *East St. Louis Monitor, St. Louis American, Poetry from the Masters, St. Louis Muse, St. Louis Sentinel, Alestle, Tambourine, Free Lance, Negro Digest, Sacramento Bee, Sacramento Observer, Sacramento Union, Drumvoices Revue, Sou'wester, Oberlin Review, East St. Louis Journal, Essence Magazine, St. Louis Post-Dispatch*.

Cover and Interior layout by Relana Johnson
Front cover photograph by Eugene B. Redmond

For the Arkansippians,
All Kin & Kindred Lovers & Warriors,
All Inhabitants of the Word,
Familistically

Mother: Emma Jean (Hutchinson) Redmond. Circa 1940s.
Father: John Henry Redmond, Sr. 1968.

In gratitude: Loretta Dumas for typing the corpus of this book and providing decades-length inspiration and support; Alfred Henderson II, former student/now editorial assistant for various projects—too numerous to mention—associated with "Memwars"; my niece Roslyn Redmond for typing portions of the MS for this book; Bettie Clay for "closure" assistance in preparing "Memwars" for submission to publisher; and Maya Angelou, sister-friend of forty years running, for opening her Winston-Salem (NC) home to me for twelve summers running—a "wood shed" of green solace where I crafted many of these poems and partook of her "welcome table."

Contents

Section Five
Songs From an Afro/Phone (*Early 1970s*)

Section Eight
Long Distance Warriors, Dreamers & Rhymers (*1980s to 2010***)**

Introduction

With the publication of *Arkansippi Memwars*, Third World Press is honored to continue the forty-five-year-old legacy that established a new context for cultural exploration and tongued a new language for its discussion. This collection, spanning five decades of Eugene B. Redmond's literary life, represents only a portion of the contributions he has made to the larger artistic/literary community. *Memwars*, a carefully selected expanded volume of poetry (with occasional chants and prose), reintroduces Redmond to his core audience, while at the same time, broadens his reach to newer, younger readers—ready to be schooled in poetics Redmond-style.

Rightfully named the Poet Laureate of East St. Louis, Illinois, Redmond chronicles, through verse interactions, all manner of remembrances and historical milestones. With the wide vision of an ambassador-extraordinaire, he shares the personal/other voice of the African American experience.

When asked, how he saw his literary contribution and cultural work, Redmond reflected upon a statement that he shared about another milestone achievement:

> The other day, Third Whirl Literary Guru Ishmael Reed, one of the founders of the Before Columbus Foundation/American Book Awards, phoned to tell me why I was being given the 2012 ABA (my second one after 1993) for Lifetime Achievement: "Congratulations on your latest 'impressive (!)' achievement (a 700-page special issue of *Drumvoices Revue*) and for training three generations of writers." Hadn't seen it in quite that way.

But now that I think of it...as of December 1, I will enter my 75th year in the breach & breadth—in the forests—of poetrees. Seven & a half decades of straddling "w/rituals" re: multifarious struggles thru percussive arts (jazzgasms)—& the art of raising good grief & hell, conch/us/nest & East Boogie* pedagogy re: Henry (Ankh) Dumas Soulos, Habitation Madame Katherine Dunham, East Saint Milesville, Jackie (Joyner-Kersee) Junction, Amos "Leaping Leon" Thomas's Yodel Village, Barbara Ann—"20 trips-to-Africa"—Teer, prepping for/steering EBR Riders & Writers, ditto for daughter Treasure & my other "familistic" treasures.

None of it could have dropped without buckets of coal & buckets of blood, tambourines & holy rollers, Baptists & Seventh Day Adventists—w/those Afro-biblical bi-labials, sibilants & fricatives; w/out railroad tracks & smoke stacks, slaughtering houses & other killing floors, a purring mother who called my father "Mr. Redmond," two jazzaic/blues-head big brothers—John ("Red") Henry Jr. & Burnett (Bunny)—among 8 siblings, & a grand wise grandmother** who thought I wouldn't live to be 21 due to "mannishness" in the face of "white folks." In long, it's been a familistic souljourn.

This "musing" which was printed in the *The St. Louis American* on October 4, 2012 encapsulates the didactic depth and daring Eugene B. Redmond has come to define through the presence/presents of word, page, and thought. *Arkansippi Memwars* firmly validates his place as a literary giant. Read his work, internalize his language, understand his path and celebrate with us as we celebrate his seventy-fifth year—and another beginning.

---

*Nickname for East St. Louis
**Rosa Ann Quinn—1880-1969

SECTION ONE
From East Saint Arkansippi
to Southeast Asia

EBR and Marine Corps buddy. Jacksonville, Florida. 1958

Blackfest

for East Saint Arkansippi Homeys

Amidst ample helpings of snow,
    We break wood & lumps of coal, repair socks & souls,
Light candles & kerosene lamps,
    Brim with homework & biblical verses,
Inhale kitchen sauces "collard" with greens, until . . .
    African nightfires dance & cackle/dance & cackle,
& our neon bodies are Kwanzaa/Xmas Trees
    Brushing against walls of the dark . . .
Now, children of the *whirl*,
    Come! Congregate, shed sweat with us,
& *swirl swirl swirl swirl* . . .

The Eye in the Ceiling

for Gerald E. Thomas and Donald L. Finkel

You sit snug in my ceiling
Staring at the room
While insects worship you.

But I can hide you in the night
And your body like a corpse
Loses its heat in seconds.

This time however
Resurrection is simple,
Far simpler than the painful
Mathematics of your birth:

Though in your final death
I'll go through the clumsy
Ritual of unwinding you,

Knowing I could not
Have touched you
In your citadel an hour ago.

Sea Changes: Recalling 1958-1960

He's a deep sea diver with a stroke that can't go wrong.
—Bessie Smith, "Empty Bed Blues"

mariners in waiting, we swam
Midwestern/mid-century scapes
between deceptively glossy seas:
Ethiopian cum *Atlantic* behind us
& *Califia's* restive *Pacific* ahead.

just cocky recruits sparring with fear
& trailing the First Middle Passengers
by several generations, we were released
from the holds of grave-deep
swimming holes, mini-seas,
lush luster lakes & brown breasted
river towns rife with barges, railroads
& slaughter houses chugging,
clacking & belching blues.

we stroked Far West
(enroute to Far East)
past oval-, horse shoe- & snake-
shaped water bodies,
cloud shot mountains, dizzy deserts,
a Vegas Oasis, beauty-
full & ominous canyons
grand as oceans of produce—
before boot-camping on banks
of a mythic *San Diego Sea*, just above
the *Sea of Cortez*, be-
coming licitly lethal infant trees:
bayonet-bearing *grunts* & *semper fi* doo-woppers,
cooks & snipers, cryptographers & compasses & pathfinders,
helicopters & vessels/

cruise-ready to criss-cross claustrophobic wide open nests:
Phillipine Sea, Formosan Strait, Sea of Japan, South China Sea
& endless shadows wading thru shallow-water rice farms.
buoyed by the Golden Dragon's Domain
(at the 180th meridian), we undulated
in the embrace of a sea-wide hammock:
a lovely, deadly sweet-sweet silently bleating blue
where I wrote love letters to six sibling sisters—&
mermaids—back home in "East Saint Louis toodle-oo."

Barbequed Cong: Or We Laid My Lai Low

at My Lai we left lint for lawns
feathered with frameless wingless birds,
barbequed and bodyless heads of hair
hanging from the charcoal gazes of burnt huts.

rice-thin hides harbored
flesh-flailing pellets,
unregenerative crops trigger-grown from the trunks of
        branchless
mechanical trees.
as barbeque grills grew hotter, with ghost-hot heat
mothers cooked children and causes
in grease of blood-glazed breasts,
resigned in the weighty whisper that:
"one can only die once."

II

cannon cut My Lai into fleshy confetti.
pellet-potted half cooked carcasses curing in rice wine.
(rat tat-tat of an idea. souvenirs for patron-saints presiding
        over oil wells.)
flat-faced down in the mud like some unclaimed unnamed
        yet undreamt dream.
while miniature machine-gun minds
mate with mole-holes
on the muddy highways of swamp or swampless night.

III

"Westward, Whore!"
hear ye...hear ye:
a declaration of undeclared causes.
a preamble to constipation and conscription.
dare we overcome?
even arrive?
slightly begin?
go forth against grains before mornings unfold?

IV

my lands! My Lai!
puppet shows and portable pentagods soar or sneak from
        Saigon.
Shine came on deck of the mind this morning and said:
"there's a sag in the nation's middle.
which way extends the natal cord—
north or south?"

i lay down my life for My Lai and Harlem.
i lay down my burden in Timbuktu, East Saint Loo and
Baltimore.
we waited long and low
like low-strung studs for My Lai
when we reared and rammed her
with spark-sperm spitting penises—
then withdrew westward 6000 miles
(a pacific coffin of the mind between us)
to vex canned good consciences
and claim the 5th Amendment.

1963: Kwansaba for "10ᵗʰ Street Tech"

We were mere hyper-active students, debatin'
Nuclear War & Civil Rights, Greek Drama
& Women's Lib, MLK's Big March &
JFK's New Frontier, *The Other America* &
Catch 22—until bullets, raining on Kennedy
in Dallas, drained East Saint Louis of
its Light—but what did we know?

Section Two

Sentry of the Four Golden Pillars
1960s

Malcolm X (right) and Clyde C. Jordan (EBR's mentor). In East St. Louis. 1962.

Sacred Place

In all sacred places: Brooklyn,
East St. Louis,
Cleveland,
Ibadan,
Watts,
Harlem,
Chicago,
Abijan,
Philly
...jazzography is a serious
religion.

Professors,
Teachers,
Audiences
Study invisibly-hooded holymen:
Duke, Bird, Brown, those Milestones who scatted
Drum-ready from African, then New Orleans, loins.

The bandstand/is the altar/
No one blasphemes.
Not even my woman who/
Kneels reverently with me
Each week and/claims
Not to "Understand."

Smoke and Fire

for "Smokey" Bill Robinson

No standards can gage
This soul-laden airblade;
Poet that makes pain pleasing.

Medicine man from Motown,
Mixing multi-phonic brown,
Rhythmic Sun Ra on the ground—
Tonal bridge to Africa!

Controlled lyric.
Luscious orchestration
Embodied in boyish voice
& beige frame:
Millennia of the strained of the strongest winds
Stripped to a decade of tonal timber.

Baldwin of voice!
The ladies' choice!

Hallelujahs vexed by secular hymns
Hatched and hurled
Through the steeply deep resonance
Of blues sermons.

Love Necessitates

Grandmother's love
Was sometimes her wrath:
    Quick caresses with switch or ironing cord.

My young unhoned hide knew
Volcanic
Voodoo
Vengeance:
Sting-swift payment for unperformed errands and orders;
Rod and wrath for tarrying too long under Black Bridge.

One did not sass Grandma,
Whose love was *gleam* and *steam:*
Precise preparation (mercy!)
For the Academy of Hard Knocks.

Last Night

Last night,
The stars scrambled
To one corner of the sky
And chorused
My thoughts
Drenched in rain
Beneath a street lamp.

I was embarrassed:
Knowing they knew
Those thoughts
And of you.

But absent of shame,
I was later
Chaka, Zulu-zealous,
Dancing
Through jungle traffic lights,
Spear-tearing the night to claim
Your swells and swerves.

Your voice—which came to me
From the darkness—
Died out in even tones
As a pillow met my face
And a knock at the door
Assassinated my dream.

The Bum

Often dogs smell
And track him, as he
Creeps along clean
Alleys,
And hears
Among other things
The clash of cocktail
Glasses
On patios.

From tin chalices
He
Devises secret
Menus
And borrows
Week-old news.

And sometimes,
The silent eyes
Of patrol cars
Seek out his
Private feast.

In a pillow of heap,
Near the dump,
The moon hides is
The wilderness
Of his dreams.
And a falling star
Is the brightest
Sun he knows.

My Study is a Battleground

Each knell of the clock
Hounds my growing rage.

And the unfaithful pen
Lies Silent,
Refusing to birth
Dark Symbols
Dancing in the
Womb of my brain.

Wedge Wall, Huge Hand
Leffingwell & Franklin Avenues, St. Louis, MO

for Luther Mitchell, the Rev. Charles Koen,
Sam Petty, and Percy Green

I

Walls usually obstruct, disrupt
Or hold things up—
Rarely are they pathways to pride and power
Like St. Louis' WALL OF RESPECT,
Black/Built so Blacks can see their (Blackness) tower.

The WALL is a huge hand out-stretched
Or
Turned
On
Its
Edge
Toward the caged overcast;
A hard hand whose horoscopes
Criss-cross
Or
Run parallel in time
3000-years-backwards-in-the-mind;

A hallowed hand
Blood-stained in BLACK BRICK,
Etchings
Of
Unearned
Agony.

See: Black people passing by;
Younger girls stop and sigh;
Brick-by-brick the faces rise;
Stare, stunned, the stolen eyes.

Ending its day-long glance,
The swollen sun splurges a final stare—
Its stiletto eye having baked bone-hard
The painted faces in the
Skillfully-sculpted hand.

Mounting ladders and platforms
Black artists,
Their solemn sacred tools singing in silence,
Apply pride/pain.

From the valley of asphalt and garbage cans
An uneven line of eyes,
Some leaning against iron knees,
Watch artists moving like
Ancient Egyptian laborers paralyzing sand into
Magnificent faces of Egyptian pyramids.

III

The WALL?
Curiosity turned to reverence!
The ungraspable
Grasped;
Towering, untouchable,
Over timid stares of the "enemy."

Eye-for-an-eye
For each passerby,

Wooer of wine-washed sidewalks,
The WALL is the people
Is the WALL is
A Whale WALL.

Strikingly still at a vigorous pace;
A haggard beard or a violent face;
Cold, angered stares or a bonnet with lace;
Or Garvey's warm urge: "Up You Mighty Race!"

WALL belongs to the peopleBLACK,
Who come to it,
Like Moslems to Mecca—
Wrested, finally, by truth from colder walls
That dope their minds and give
Them a white Jesus to die for.

The WALL winds miles Miles s/miles Miles...
As the steel-knuckled fists jut
Like street lamps along the way.

The Assassin

Remembering Malcolm, Martin, and Fred Hampton

America's bastard
Child
Peers down the skinnysteel neck
Of a lightning rod whose
Only
Eye
Spits forth fiery acorns of iron
That turn dreams to dung
Hills where
        dictators grow.
devils dabble with death.
            "dreams"
            draw
            destruction.
And the spiritual architects of
Such unsportsmanlike conduct
            sound false alarms
            from an alabaster
                castle
                in D.C.

All A-Thighed in Black

for Earth Mother

She had a "wicked walk,"
Was well a-thighed,
A luscious,
Ripe
Juicy
Moving
Groovin'
Black-grape-of-a-woman.

And the poet pondered pounds of thighs,
Jungles of thighs that bend like branches
And give forth juice.

Black women have thighs
And eyes that press against
The mind (despite prisons of girdles and adhesive dresses).

Brown
Beige
Tan
Black: thick-thin-throbbing
Eyes and thighs.
Eyes that thigh and thighs that eye.
Thighs of gregarious spring green,
Growing hedges, rippling like bread-baked-brown,
Topped with black-lip softness.
Ovens that heat and scorch
And singe souls.
Thighs that quiver (like liver) and upset nerves.
Thighs of noise and oil, sweat and slaps—

Power and passion and pain, plain and prime,
Of motion (less) . . . quietly shrinking or swelling,
Swaying or swooning.

Thighs that thigh
And thighs that sigh.
Thighs that cry and
Thighs that lie.

Wide thighs, wise as winter,
Knowing many things—after having been
Bathed in themselves,
Honed in the oil from their captive oasis
And brought to high sheens by the come of lovers.

Black women have "thighs that agonize eyes."

In a Time of Rain and Desire

for anysomeplaceone

      a wind-geared cloud of flesh
rained desire into the shiny
rivers of your face:
      and turned your arching cheeks into
shores dew-damped and dazzle-dark;
      and milk-glazed your twin-mountains
nippled with brown berries;
      and liquid-pebbled your tributaries
known as legs;
      and overflowed into that pond
(south of your navel and east and west of your thighs)
gripped in grass and precious as the holy (wholee) grail.

and this cloud is lost forever
in the forest of your biology.

Parapoetics

for my former students and writing friends in East St. Louis, Illinois

Poetry is an *applied science:*
Re-wrapped corner rap;
    Rootly-eloquented cellular, soulular sermons.

    Grit reincarnations of
    Lady Day
    Bird
    & Otis;
    Silk songs pitched on 'round and rhythmic rumps;
    Carved haloes (for heroes) and asserted maleness:
    Sounds and sights of fire-tongues
    Leaping from lips of flame-stricken buildings
       in the night.

    Directions: apply poetry as needed.
    Envision.
    Visualize.
    Violate!
    Shout!
    Right words.
    Rite!!
    Cohabitate.
    Gestate.
    Inpregnate your vocabulary.
    Dig, a parapoet!

Parenthesis: Replace winter with spring, move Mississippi
    to New York, Oberlin (Ohio) to East St. Louis, Harlem
    to the summer whitehouse. Carve candles and flintstones
    for flashlights.

Carry your poems.
Grit teeth. Bear labor-love pains.
Have twins and triplets.
Fertilize poem-farms with after-birth,
Before birth and dung (rearrange old words);
Study/strike tradition.

Caution to parapoets.
Carry the weight of your own poem
...it's a *heavy lode.*

Spearo's Blues (Or: Ode to a Grecian Yearn)

A soliloquy in seven parts

I

I can't hear myself think in America no more!
With the specter of Vietnams at our own front door!

II

The dark'nin threat from within is dissent.
But that ain't what Tom Jefferson meant.
(Caesar wouldn't've dug it at all, yall!)

III

That's why I'm shooting for 'Mars' by A.D. 2000.
(Aside: I may get back to D.C. before then if
the light years are limp and long.)

IV

With the muse on my mailing list,
Green lights and bouquets from Barry,
Dick's (groping-gripping) gracious silence,
(Alas, though I hear his thoughts through a
bug in his floor: *"I remember when I was an
unemployed schizoid."*),
Ky Kentucky Fried and in the Colonial Casket,
Cleaver neatly collected and exiled in paperback,
Me neo-naked in tamed tunic
(a real Ulyssean cock!),
The Parthenon's a stone's throw
From Pillars of Pennsylvania Avenue.

V

The mouth's the message: Think later.
Besides, you're in quick-draw country.
(cf..., Barry's Law.)

VI

(Aside: Anyway, cultureless America's a long
Way from Athens (Ohio) or Olympus. *It's the I.Q.*
that counts.)

VII

And now, yellow Americans,
Tradition is what this country needs.
What? What? (cupping the ear)

Finis

Observer: "I hear the wail of a tenor-troubled anglo-sax.
And from among the dung, a silent tongue is rung:
'Bring hue and crew
Take cue from Agnew
And do this in remembrance of Joe McCarthy!'"

Exiled in Buffalo

in a mourning sea of lackadaisical language
poetry becomes the pain i pirate
after a night whose song I sang
among multitonal shadows of lorraine

now I listen to those shadows
above hiss and drone and roar of alien hotel shower.
she sleeps, then leaps into day from a night
that I promise to recreate in a poem

as a pirate, i am a carloadoflove laden, also, with deep melodic
urgency.
it is true:
"i can love,"
i say,
as I hurry
to alter courses and events . . . .

Inter-American Writers Congress, Buffalo, New York, 1969

Disneyland

On Sundays
I sometimes ride past plush pastures
And snug suburban burial grounds:
The dead—and animals—live better than the *living*.

Cool comfortable green blankets & carpets for coffins and
      cows.
Disneyland for the dead: mansions of mausoleums;
Quiet statuesque status-stone and marble.
(TV commercial comes into relief: *America's Marlboro man
      heaves hay from helicopter to snow-bound beef.*)

Over ghettos, fallout is the frappe of the daily diet
Of sulfur & carbon. (Skinny rats and roaches are scarce
as ebony in the ivory house.)
And on our asphalt safari, we hunt big game
Of hungry maggot and overnourished pig.

While across town,
Ladies gray and grave as gravy
Ponder man's fate at their monthly meeting:

"Should cats and dogs wear clothes?"

Inseedent

At the lowest
levels
of the unlit,
I surround a sun-bomb
with a wreath of idols and ideas . . .

my mind explodes
and casualties
of
thoughts
lie mangled
decomposed
on civilization's frayed floor.

Wind Goddess: Sound of Sculpture

for Doris Mayes (Mezzo-Soprano), after March 17, 1970
Recital, Conservatory, Oberlin College

In *Beulahland!*
You highly stand.

Raped wind-hordes
Walled & wailing against *unforgotten* gates
At your back.

Meticulously led,
These rough airs
Come sculpted,
Amplified,
Like African arrows,
From the silky camouflaged turbulence
& beauty of your middlecountry.

Here is no sun-forsaken soul,
As that ancient light leaps
& smiles its rainbow of sounds
From your—
Now choiric/ancestral
Then epic/soulo—
Voice,
Vexing cured chant, and . . .
"Everytime I feel the spirit . . . ."

Definition of Nature

In this stoned and
Steely park,
Love is an asphalt
Fact:
  flowers
  birds
  trees
  rushing or creeping brooks
are framed on walls and tv tubes.

But each night when the city shrinks,
  the stars roof us,
And any bush becomes
  our Bantu wonderland.

The Fallen Alto

In a junk heap
I saw you
Muzzled by a tin can,
Your stained,
Twisted self
No longer
Weaving life from
Course winds
Filtering
Through
A dozen nostrils
And one gaping mouth.

In your
Breathless
But unsunken frame
Insects dwell
And cocoons cling.
You create still!

Would your
Master,
Left voiceless
By your old age,
Know you now?

Strong Lines

Love lines will last—
From tribal rival
To funnels and tunnels
Of the oldest mind.

Lines etch,
Arrow, narrow through
As lines must.

Lines will last,
Last—
Elastify to include
Martin and Eldridge
In the same stretch.

Lines defy, furrow, infer
More lines in all directions:
Solar biology,
Bodies of water,
Unlocked lands,
Royalty and riffraff,
Ebony and mulatto,
Palm-readings,
Longitude and latitude,
Spinal columns and raised buttocks.

Lines will last,
Encage,
Care for,
Until the day of battle.

SECTION THREE
Consider Loneliness as These Things
Late 1960s

EBR: Reading by lamplight. Okinawa, Japan. 1959.

Consider Loneliness as These Things

Consider loneliness as a lull,
As some secret space that jails the mind,
As a circumstantial melody: the blues of
Wretchedness or the blues of joy;
As some totem of penitence or pity or pride,
Sagging from the neck like a lead medallion
Or a dead bird:
Spinning out,
Spinning out wire-threads or hardfeathers of confinement;
As a hypnotist, eye-blind, with psychic sight
And strength to unleash the lances of unexpurgated pain,
Of unquelled thought-quakes, or Watusi-tall dreams.
Consider loneliness as these things.

Consider loneliness as a weaver of want,
As a giver of needs undefined,
As some ancestral repository
For a personal mythic tablet;
As a nerve, nudged overgently—
Or laced with worry;
As a womb, wailing out its
Liquid waifs, its tight lips waiting,
Waiting...
As a tyrant, timeless and elastic—
Consider loneliness.

Looking Through Liquid

Joy.
Envious wind gathering
       at your Himalayan thighs.

Joy.
Winding molding, cone-shaping
       vieing for v-shaped prize.

Joy.
Serene self-of-yourself bonelessly
       limp at chilled sunrise.

Joy.

Sundowning

Clouds fall upwards like splashed ink
Against the sky.

Which is moving:
The car or the world?

The day cools.
Our brains stop boiling.
And evening refrigerates our thoughts.

You descend upon me with the night chill,
Peripatetic and omni-dark.

I drive one-handed.
You match point with number on radio,
Mumble celestial jargon in my ear,
And flip my fly zip
Back and forth.

Radio,
Road hum,
Leering lights careen on
Fender and forehead.
Face and Foreskin.
Your eyes spheres of fire!
Do you work some
African magic on me?

Second Coming

Fire! Fire!
Where, oh where, will you be
When flames go on that global spree?

When Earth's crotch and crop catch fire
And the planets won't piss on the pyre?
But wait for echoes from the ashen urn:
"Oh didn't it, didn't it burn!
Oh, my Lord, didn't it burn!"

When a sleazy planet shaken from nap
         Asks,
"Burn? Burn? Oh dear, has earth got the clap?"

Carryover

Thinking about Jimmy Dixon, Clarence Nelson, and Darnell Sullivan

I have been tattooed for life:

A thought called EAST ST. LOUIS

Is etched into each Island of my Brain.

EAST ST. LOUIS will rise!

Will rise from the muddy gutty Mississippi.

Will rise disguised as AFRICA.

WILL RISE!

WILL RISE THROUGH THE MIND-EYES OF

hustler & hairdresser
teacher & astronaut

athlete and anchorman
mathematician and mime

waiter & dishwasher
elk & mason

cabdriver and architect
hodcarrier and cartoonist

maid & mechanic

doctor & undertaker

journalist and judge
bluesician and be-bopper

preacher & plumber
gardener & garbage collector

violinist and veterinarian
griot and gutbucketeer

EAST SAINT ain't dead yet!

I've got the scars and tattoos to prove it!

Can't you feel the yeast in the air!

The Atmosphere is Starving

Moon tune.
Spatial rhythm.
Gorgeous galaxy.
Otherwhereness.
(I pity emptiness of
space or stomach.)

Song of the ether:
Feathery phonics for speeding phallic
Splitting molecular madness.
The universe has no more cherry
And Harlem no more food.

Moon tune.
Coal-dust colored faces
Copper coat the night.
"Might is right!"

Spaceship: gouge through malnutrient
Stomachs; let no lord of testament
Cause you lag.
(What is the formula for manufacturing man?)

Moon: don't waste the milk of the cow that mounts you.
Moon tune: 24 billion leagues above the sea
(and still unanchored and unsung).

Forgive this rude intestinal growl
Interrupting your congressional symphony.

High Gloss

Painted poetry,
One has to admit,
Is cute, rather patent-leatherish
And unabused by social refuse.

Church neatly separated from state,
Kinship lines unconnected,
No emotion except
For flowers and the plight of flies,
(Politics don't exist!)

Whitened lines withstand weight
Of age and order;
History's corridor is no narrower
Than the minds that make it,
Unstained, unblamed by acidic
Or inelegant utterances.
(Nobody peed in nunneries
and little children don't have
sex organs.)

Painted poetry is a ritual of order:
All things ascend, descend
But never criss-cross.
There is unshaken shape,
Unbroken rules, unfailing form—
And no human foible.

Little People

In the omen-cloaked chill
Of the October wind,
Brittle little legs snap, crackle and bend
But never crumble.
Books, grasped in belts and boxes,
Are pulled reluctantly along
Like low-land cows after grazing.

Cool Black cavaliers, their struts
Developed to 9-year perfection, glory be!,
Apply the precision of Bo-jangles
To jubilant jaunts.

Moon children confronting late dawn:
Night people streaming to meet the sun;
Sunrise on sunset's hindparts,
Carcass of the moon, the day carts.

Little people don't contrive,
Contribute to,
War—they just inherit it.

The World's Well

After hatred for lunch
Seeing mamma degraded in factory washroom cartoon,
Snide white eyes on the homebound bus,
Obscenities on the 6 o'clock news,
This ain't the blues,
I conclude:

The world's well!
Except for chronic constipation,
An occasional nosey nation,
And Western plantations.
The world wanders as worlds will.
And the ghosts from its several deaths
Haunt roots of rivers.
All things exist!

Including hatred of heart or hand,
Love of lord or land.
All things will do as all things must:
Condition, predicament, precept notwithstanding.
As I go on like I must.

The Fire Inside

Whether the weather is windy or rainy,
Stormy or sane with average sun,
I express some eastern elation at creation;
I express distress (sometimes) at my inability
To dispel the mental pell-mell of
                    Heaven or Hell
Or the knife of life.

These things, however, cause me no prolonged
Strife, especially since I know they
Do not phase the African.
Besides, I tell myself, my understanding
Ancestors will forgive me
For such sacrilegious thought:
Bought albeit with western currency.

Each day, I trace strand: lines along hand and land.
Whence came I?

A change in weather is rather well accepted
After wind has awakened and unwound my ethnic
Consciousness and I am too much with Africa.
Lord! Lord!

SECTION FOUR

River of Bones and Flesh and Blood
Late 1960s to Early 1970s

Henry Dumas, William Davis, Eugene B. Redmond. Young teacher-counselors at SIU-East St. Louis's Experiment in Higher Education. 1967.

River of Bones and Flesh and Blood
Mississippi

For Doris Cason

River of time:
Vibrant vein,
Bent, crooked,
Older than the Red Men
Who named you;
Ancient as the winds
That break on your
Serene and shining face;
One time western boundary of America
From whose center
Your broad shoulders now reach
To touch sisters
On the flanks

River of truth: Mornings
You leap, yawn 2000 miles,
And shed a giant joyous tear
Over sprouting, straggling
Hives of humanity;
Nights you weep
As the moon, tiptoeing
Across your silent silky
Face, hears you praying
Over the broken backs
Of black slaves who rode
Crouched and huddled
At your heart in the bellies
Of steamships.

River of Memory:
Laboratory for Civil War
Boat builders
Who left huge eyes of steel
Staring from your sullen depths;
Reluctant partner to crimes
Of Ku Klux Klansmen;
River moved to waves
Of ecstasy
By the venerable trumpets
Of Louis Armstrong,
Clark Terry
And Miles Davis.

River of Bones:
River of bones and flesh—
Bones and flesh and blood;
The nation's largest
Intestine
And longest conveyor belt;

River MISSISSIPPI
River of little rivers;
River of rises,
Sometimes subdued
By a roof of ice, descending finally
On your Southward course
To spit
Into the Gulf
And join the wrath
Of larger bodies.

Epigrams for My Father

John Henry Redmond Sr.

I

Fatherlore: papa-rites, daddyhood;
  Run & trapsong: Search & dodgesong,
Steelhammeringman,
Gunbouter; whiskeywarrior.
Nightgod!
Moonballer/brawler grown old.
Slaughterhouse/river mackman:
Hightale teller & totempoleman.

II

Wanderer across waters:
Folkbrilliance & Genuisgrit;
Railraging railsplitter:
Railrage! Railrage!
IC & BM&O & MoPac & Midnight Special:
Freight train . . . . bring my daddy back!

III

Stone-story. The story of stone, brokenbricks—
Rocks hurled in pleasure & rage,
Pebbles soft & silent:
Home-dome is a blues-hard head.

IV

45-degree hat, Bulldurham butt bailing from lips;
Gabardine shining shining shining
Above while silk socks—
    satin man
    satin man
    silksure & steelstrong
    hammerhold on life
    hammerhold on life

V

Sun-son, Stonebone. Blackblitz.
Fatherlore, Struggledeep: Afridark, Afrolark,
    Daddydepth—
    Riverbottom song.

Gods in Vietnam

Mechanical oracles
Dot the sky,
Casting shadows on the sun.
Instead of manna
Leaflets fall
To resurrect coals, dead
From the week's bombing.

Below in the
Jungle,
Flaming altars buckle under
Prophecies;
And smoke whimpers
In the west wind.

Dry seas hide the
Cringing fold
While fishermen leap from clouds,
Nets blooming on their
Lean bodies.

The sun slumps,
Full;
Before it sleeps,
Solemn chaplains come,
Their voices choked
In suspicious silence

September in March

No sun, no clouds,
And the day is
Suddenly clear.

Flat winds move like
Wide unseen walls
Against the buildings
And the people.

Skirts flutter in
Embarrassment, while
High-crown and porcupine
Hats and wing-like caps
Tumble in the streets.

On the main drag—
Extending out over numerous
Shops and stores—
Large canvas canopies
Wave and subside.

Small whirlpools can be
Seen where-ever dust and
Other particles collect.

I cannot see the wind.

City Night Storm

for L. Wendell Rivers

Dark winds kiss the walls
And split on the blades of corners;
The burning eyes of the city dance
In a thousand rusting skulls.

Twisting trees listen to
The pulses of tired streets;
And birds miss their landings.

A fleeing garbage can suddenly
Scares a sleeping cat; and a drunk,
Held upright by the headwind,
Slouches into daylight.

The condescending moon says nothing,
But coasts half-seen along night's ceiling;
And the angry, chilling breath rushes over
Darkness, like waters over a fall.

The 18 Hands of Jerome Harris

Drumsticks masturbate in his hands!
As over-sexed audiences follow suit,
Their hot flesh flinching, meanwhile, under
The patter of penis-shaped wooden feet.

18 hands sound songs of stones with dried bones!
Polished branches, baked in African blood,
Taptunes for hard times:
Hard times for babies leaping
From the beat of black bellies—
The howl of an ancient echo—
Hung in the brick-steel-glass-weedy
Throat of urban and rural jungles.

The branches have many personalities:
Heels hounding hostile pavements in search of jobs,
Fans,
Drills,
Hammers that haunt ear drums,
Whips and arrows aimed at
Sailing cymbals,
Igniting them with
Flashes from flaming eyes.

18 hands in fierce flight or pained pursuit:
Heating and bothering the delirious drums
Like a teenager who traps his ripe prey
In some dark hallway.

The branches cling fast or climb slowly
Like heavy hands of tower clocks
Announcing the day's age.

They move in Harris' hands,
Timed and intent,
Through
Prayers!
Battles!
Great bodies of blood
Driven as by daredevils
And horse-herders constantly at some finish line.

Or they tread cautiously
As hands curing animal carcasses
Dying for drums in the sun.

18 hands, holding blood-blessed branches,
Make hollow drums deep and long
Like the unwritten diaries of Katherine Dunham
Whose sacred legs still straddle continents.

The solo ends in drums of living flesh;
Applause shatters straying silence;
Later, as ladies get up to go pee
And smoldering eyes rise up to see,
The thin skin of the drums lies quivering
Like a young woman just well sanctified,
Beneath the fallen eyes and unarched shoulders
Of Jerome Harris:
Prophet of skin and tin!
Teller of tales!
Keeper of time!
Holder of blood-blessed branches!

Drummer with 18 hands!

Spring in the Jungle

You tiptoed
Naked
Into the
Jungle
Of my soul;

And the underbrush
Divided before
You.

A choir of birds
Grew
Understandably
Silent;

And I stood
Beside
Myself with joy
And watched
The season grow
To
Spring

Let my soul
Be always
Green
And sprinkled with
Daisies;

Let there be
Dew for the sun to bathe in
And winds to do rituals
For the
Moon.

Twilight

Her *mojo* dimmed to a mutter
Her *firehead* shaved of its flames
Her *bloodpace* slowed to a crawl
Her *magic* brimming with names
Her *queenquilts* trimmed to a shawl
Her *lightning* chilled to a flicker
Her *power* calmed to a call

Invasion of the Nose

for Joseph Harrison

His nose was his radar,
His eyes icy darts that moved faster than speed-of-sound
        Jets
He could rap like a pneumatic drill!
Or croon like Smokey Bill when the occasion arose.

He was a cool,
Hip,
OFF-INTO-A-THING dude,
Mellow—
In yellow silk undershirts
Exposed through unbuttoned
Jerseys from Greenfields.

"Dig this, man," he would say,
"I ain't tripping with no jive-ass-bitch."

He stood/hung/laid/dealt
On the corner,
Bent in a 20-degree angle,
One hand clutching the wrist
Of the opposite arm behind his back.
And he could dart-like-lightning
Into a 5 ft. female's ear.

His popping-tongue titillated the titties
Of other men's wives
And awed adolescent girls;
Middleaged ladies gave him
Fat-fees for his flailing fingers.
He was an acknowledged action eater
Who was hip to *Trane,*

Bird,
Prez,
Jug Head,
Duke,
Count,
Ray Charles, James Brown and *Howlin' Wolf.*

But one day
She found a hole in his soul,
Put a fertile fang in his thang

And his nose grew like blunderbuss barrels.

Black Community: Mind & Mirror

I
Mind
Got a boogaloo in your brain!
—K. Curtis Lyle

Take *long* breaths & strides,
Stroke & straddle an ocean:
       Sitting—thinking—running
Thru the book of *yourself.*
The book of the dead
The living & the *yestermorrow.*

To the sky's skull
To the earth's belly-center
To the eyeballs of oceans
To the tonsils of birds & storms
To the navel of the sun
Stroke-stroke-stroke-stroke
Full strength to what Stevie Wonder called
"Yester-you" & *"Yester-me";*

To *self,* sunk deep in blues and praise songs of the mind,
Cuddled in the applauding waves of that *last river,*
Brooding in a battlefield named memory,
Thumping in a motherdrum called Africa,
Styling in a footstomp, banjoboogie, tambourine,
       boogaloo & *mood indigo,*
Swelling in a socket or pocket or rocket of earth
Where unbranded brains think sea-size thoughts:
       In a book of song!
       In a book of dance!
       In a book of style!

In an air-sea where stars caucus
In a mind-act
In a mobile-thought
In the armor & shield of ancestral corridors
In the hooves of ideas prancing & dancing in the mirror of
       the multitude!
Take *long* breaths & strides,
Stroke & straddle an ocean:
      An ocean of song!
      An ocean of dance!
      An ocean of style!
Sitting—thinking—running
Thru the book of *yourself,*
Thru the book of the dead, the living
& the *yestermorrow.*

II

Mirror

Mirages of the mind rend,
      Sometimes send mad,
The mirrors of the soul:
But way shape form & fashion
      Come, *spirit-driven,*
From glossy black forests:
"This little light of mine . . . I'm gonna let it *shine!*
      Let it *shine!*
      Let it *shine!*
      Let it *shine!*

Lance-like *yestermirrors* of toil, tall tales & talismen,
Of mojo-men and sledgehammering horrors,

Of glassy grease & the sweat of unswum rivers to cross.
Of spear-dash glint & the razor-rove of eyes;
From the massforehead comes:

Lucid light!
Oh luminescence of the soul!
Yestermirrors illuminate the soul of song,
Illuminate the *self,* sunk deep in *Black Gloss,*
Deep in licorice lacquer, deep in the throb-photo of
   daddydrum;
Night arches into Africa:
  Sounds are drawn . . . oh ebony mirror!
  Sounds are drawn . . . oh beams to bear!
  Sounds are drawn . . . oh night shellacked!
This *mirror,* this *mantel:* light-lances bouncing from
   foreheads & halls,
Rebounding, resounding in the bellybutton of the drum:
Clatter of ghetto teeth, clicks of tongues,
Ancestral echoes, songs of dust & hurt, bluesful rime:
   acoustical *mirrors!*

Yestermirrors are *yester-us* are *yestermorrows.*
  Let them shine!
  Let them shine!
  Let them shine!

Angel of Mercy

For Angela Yvonne Davis,
a performance piece—voice/s and drum/s

for if they take you in
the morning they will be coming
for us that night.

—James Baldwin

Trials! Trials!
Another *trial!*
Another trial to the trek towards Sun-center
Towards Sun-song and Son-song and Songhay
Towards *yestermorrow.*

AngelAngelAngelAngel*Angela*:

>   anvil & arrow
>   anvil & arrow
>   anvil & arrow
>   Anviling & arrowing wind into *word*: impaled on the
>   pitchfork of urgency!
>   (America is a pitchfork!)

African winds/words call & caucus your co-queens:

>   *Shango's wives*
>   *Sojourner Truth*
>   *Harriet Tubman*
>   *Mary Bethune*
>   *Katherine Dunham*
>   *Aretha Franklin*

Trials! Trials! One more river to cross!!
Angela *Our* Angel of mercy!

Angela *Our* Angel of mercy!
Angela *Our* Angel of mercy!

Word-winged warrior: thrust-thrust-thrust—
Beat back the be-robed beasts;
Fly Black flame-lances to the gates of
>*Ghana*
>*Harlem*
>*Haiti*
>*Fillmore*
>*Senegal*
>*Watts*
>*Congo*
>*Chicago*

Mojo the jelly-minded jurists!
Drop goober dust on canopies and sun-porches of their
>minds!
Thrust-thrust-thrust:
Unbroken ebony bird shuttling ancestral urgencies!

Trials! Trials!
We beat them back back back:

>*one-by-one one-by-one one-by-two-by-one-by-two*
>*one-by-one one-by-one one-by-two-by-one-by-two*
>*one-by-one one-by-one one-by-two-by-one-by-two*

(Forgive them that *deny & decry.* Pray *later* for those
>sinners.)

Trials! Trials!

Night is on trial.

Day is on trial.

Color is convicted.
Dusky skin will get you 5 to life:
        ask Marcus
        ask Malcolm
        ask Martin

Ask the Angel of Mercy!

"Electrocute all ideas!!"
"Burn& gas the thinkers!!"
"Napalm the dissenters!!"

       . . . thus spake the pentagods!

Euro-America, *once more*, saved, fairy-tale-fashion,
From the fire & brimstone of diarrhea:
From the lava of its own cavernous intestines.

Angela, Sacrifice for perennial witch-hunt.
Angela: One more river to cross;
        One more river of blood to cross;
        One more cross to anvil into a spear;
        One more steeple to shape into a sword;
        No more crosses to bear!
Angela, One more, One more, One more river to cross!!!

The Bastard

these shores, these agonies

Across the white desert
Sludges the
Bastard,
His Black face upstaging
Night
As he weeps into the
Cold
Ears of a father.

On his brow
Lie stillborn the hopes
Of 3 centuries
And on the face of his
Citizen-brothers
The rebuttal.

Beside the oasis,
Mother offers a
Sword
To his burning
Tongue
While Old World orphans cast
Lot
For his inheritance.

Poetic Reflections Enroute to, and During, the Funeral and Burial of Henry Dumas, Poet, May 1968

I

Flight to New York

I am ready to die
—Henry Dumas in *Our King Is Dead*

A passive sea of white foam.
Separates this swift and fleshless bird
From the black earth that waits for *Henry Dumas, poet.*
At 30,000 feet up
The mind has plenty of space to wander:

Just think!
A second-story world—
No steps, no ladders.
Meanwhile onto aluminum-covered wings the sun leaps
And breaks into a thousand heated needles
As my head averts,
With a twist,
Its stabbing, staring presence.

Now we soar through angry winds,
Bouncing unpredictably like a football
Turned loose in some smooth, open place.
But the pilot guides the bird cautiously
Through the ordeal while our hearts,
At first hung like anxious medallions around our necks,
Resume their natural places;
And the cries, before dignifiedly choked,
Die forever in our throats.

We the living:
Are we some majestic, royal party?
A high tribunal judging the lower world?
Gods? Goddesses?
Who is above and who is below?
. . . the pilot's voice and then
A view of Staten Island.
We nose through the second sea to caress LaGuardia Field.
The stewardess smiles at the passenger sitting
Alone in the rear: "Pretty good landing in the rain,
      wasn't it?"
She's a company girl, the poet muses—a robot with nice
      legs.
Parts and rhythms of the painful puzzle fall together on the
      ground.
But I must hurry to the funeral in the Bronx.
Amid sounds and sights, I near the cab and am terrified
      at my image
In the glossy surface of its wet body.

And on the way to McCall Funeral Home
I try in vain to figure out who I am.

II
The Funeral

A Black Poet is a preacher.
—Henry Dumas

The balding black preacher
Read and ad-libbed
Before a lamp that threw
A cone-shaped light up into his face.
The eulogy was brief,
The man was eloquent and magnificent
In dark robes: *a poet saluting a poet.*

Occasionally his eyes fell
Like heavy weights
On the casket to his right,
Draped in a United States flag.
Dumas had served in the Air Force.

The articulate preacher had not known the poet
But the poet's mother.
One could see that the circumstances of the killing
Had undermined his faith.

He sought a way out: Equating the poet with "Mr.
Lincoln."
He also knew the poet wrote:

"This young man will survive
In his stories and poems," the bowed audience was
           reminded.
"He walked upright like a man . . .
There are mysteries; life is a mystery,
Death is a mystery."
The radiant black man of cloth
Was unpretentious; he broke with tradition—promising
No alternatives to death.
Seemingly unaware of heaven or hell, he suggested simply
           "a last resting place."
Those in the chapel stared intently, bleakly
Into their own thoughts.
Outside the skies cried for the dead black bard.

Forty-Five Minutes to the Cemetery

Rain,
Earlier in East St. Louis and now in New York.
The skies continue to mourn for the fallen poet and warrior,
Mojo-handler and prophet.

Four passengers in the fourth car,
Divided by a generation of intellect,
But feeling a common pain,
A mutual bewilderment:
Four gritting faces of the oppressed.

The dead poet rode in the first car
But was present in the whole train--
Smiling in approval at our candid talk.
Dumas was like that. "Man, let's just tell it," he used to say.
Yes, and he had given direction to the
Pen of the younger poet earlier that morning
Several stories up, adrift in a big bird of steel.

Our talk was shop:
"Henry and I finished Commerce High School together,"
The driver intimated.
A middleage friend of the poet's mother said:
"They're killing off all our good men; I tell ya, a black man
Today speaks his piece at the risk of losing his life."

New Yorkers talk differently than East St. Louisians,
The younger poet observed to himself.

The cars of the procession,
Standing out with bright eyes against the dim day,
Sped cautiously toward Farmingdale National Cemetery

Where white marble headstones stood mute and macabre:
Quite geometrically arranged in a sprawling well kept
        ocean of green.

Again talk: "They're slaughtering our boys in Vietnam,"
        the middleage lady
Quipped; "this graveyard will be filled up soon"
A bus carrying the Army Honor Guard joined us at the
        entrance to the cemetery.

The guard gave a trifling, sloppy salute to the fallen poet
Who had served his country.
More talk as we departed the graveside:
"Young David walks just like his daddy,"
The driver informed us about Dumas' eldest son.

"Neither of the boys understand what's going on,"
The driver's mother noted.
"Who does?" the poet asked himself.

A confession from the middleage lady: "Can't cry no more.
Just won't no more tears come out—all dried up."

Her eyes looked like aged/inquisitive rubies
Polished to worn perfection
By having seen many things
Including the dead poet's "good looking"
Remains.
The driver echoed her: "Henry was beautiful; he looked
Just like he was sleep."

The driver was a spirit lifter, also an interior observer:
"Henry thought too deep for the average person."

Upon leaving the cemetery
The procession broke up.
Cars bearing license plates from various places sped on or

turned off,
Went their way and our way.
The skies lifted their hung heads.
Mrs. Dumas smiled finally and played with her sons,
David and Michael.
The boys, cast in the same physical mold as their father,
Were impeccably dressed.

Gears of the Globe

for Gabriel Bannerman-Richter

African moon cartwheels in the night's eye;
African moon stalls in the clouds;
Black sod nods
As earth's rods,
Gears and chains
Are oiled by dewspray
And rootjuice,
Voodoo'd for another day.

Distance

I am still on fire.

The flames in my veins and heart
Boil blood and burn hissing-hot.

Yet my time is inched on
By the realization of each new
Gleam-in-a-father's-eye.

My wrinkled oval sacks
Have pumped up a sea of come
Up through a mercenary-muscle
Into vaginas, wet towels and mouths.
But each sapping of the glistening love-sauce
Creates a new supply
Like the Phoenix Bird that rises from its own ashes.

More and more, like James Brown,
I find myself saying "I used to . . . there was a time."

The mind grows younger and remembers:
The poetic but unprophetic words of my grandmother
        as she played
Tick-tack-toe on my butt with an ironing cord:
"You little black bastard; Nigger, you won't live to be 21
With your mannish tail";
Parking piously in the park to finger-fuck and poke pussy
        after dark;
Coming three times-in-a-row;
Crawling through wives' windows;
Whole weeks of whiskey and whaling without sleep:
Palating pills, inhaling hashish, sucking syrup,
And gurgling O'Grady in a 1-2-3-4 fashion.

The items mount memory's totem pole:
The wild gossip of *Lady Day;*
The trips of *Yard Bird;*
The passion and elegance of *Mr. B;*
The legacy/tragedy of *Chano Pozo;*
The hum of *Midnighters,*
Drifters,
Coasters
And *Orioles;*
The moods, minds and myths of *Miles.*

A single life,
A daily diet of death and
Under the bludgeoning of the slave drivers call
I am bound and thrown
At the feet of a white Christ
Where vultures stab and snap with putrid beaks at my
        eye balls.

I now know distance and dread:
        rivers and voices
        freedom in a cage
        freedom in a cage

Distance calls. In my secret soul heroes have always been
        Black.
But America raised me on
John Wayne
Shirley Temple
And Tarzan.

America gave me distance!
America gave me distance!

Now, while I am still on fire,
I ache in anger to get home.

Walking One Day in
Baton Rouge, Louisiana

Saturday, July 3, 1971

Walking one day in Baton Rouge,
Fresh shrimp frying in my head,
The wind suddenly gored me
In my tracks and pressed me
Against a stiff wall of air—
And, then, she was there!
Her presence an oakhold,
An ache, a gnaw, an admonishment:
Sweet teethbared arrogant
Spirit held out like a lance of hardest steel
Or a shield of wry smiles;
This presence an impaled beauty,
An impartial stare:
  And me—*with my need of nail*—
  Wanting to hit so hard it hurt.
Here in this flamespace,
The loving/loathing daydream,
My teeth and tongue boiling in butterflavored spit,
Windwalls so thick so thrustful:
  And me—*with my need of nail*—
  Wanting to hit so hard it hurt.
And the wind, treasonous and triumphant,
It pressed me to my tracks—like a slow-sucking quicksand
  And me—*wanting to hit so hard it hurt.*

Grandmother

Thinking of Rosa A. Quinn, an "Arkansippian"

Winter, 1966

She is a child
Whose dark eyes no longer
Divine the hidden fever
Or fathom rough lies
On a little black face.

Sullen walls,
Once haunted by stained
Portraits of Christ,
Are dusty monuments
To her silent desertion.

A pair of callous knees
Record four-score years
Of daily soliloquies
Chanted into
An arch of scaly hands.

And she unstops no more
The choked sewer
In the sunken street;
Nor sandbags in the rain
Mud threatening her *four o'clocks.*

Muscles that used to saw
And fashion logs into quilt-trees
Now sag
Like her long since
Shrunken breasts.

She is a strange child at 86;
Who relishes the taste of peppermint
And the somber-sugar hum of *spirituals.*

Section Five
Songs From an Afro/Phone
Early 1970s

EBR. Studio. Recording the album Bloodlinks and Sacred Places.
Heavenly Studios. Sacramento, California. 1973.

take the sculptor who carves a mask . . . while this sculptor carves, he sings a song, he sings a poem and he weaves a poem. And there you see the significant and the significance. The image and the idea in symbiosis . . . the tradition of the word-word . . . priests and artists must have the gift of imagery, of symbolism, of rhythm.

—Leopold Sedar Senghor
President of Senegal, Poet and
Philosopher of Negritude

Brothersong:
Composition for My Mirror

for John Henry Redmond Jr.

I

Dear mirror:
Dearer mirror . . . shatterless glass;
Shining and shouting back my me/my me;
Autobiography caught in nostalgic corners of mind light;
In the needelight of the son; in the lasergrace
Of the sun: kinetic kin-note,
Life-lunging lyric,
Ringdancer and Hatmaker;
Mani/gear knuckled, buckled,
Fastened, seatbelted
Onto a boldshouldered manblade.

II

Dear mirror:
Coming, humming clearer to me;
Whose brown body is a song
Whose brown body is a slug
Halfhumming halfwhisting "One Mint Julep":
"One early moanin'
While I was wawking . . ."
Mansong on a morning of shutters and chillbumps;
Bluesbalm percolating a morning of potbellies:
"Coal-l-l Man! Coal-l-l-l!
Coal-l-l Man! Coal-l-l-l!"

Dear mirror:
BeBopping "Bird" digger;
Grinding against Miles Music
As waiter, as mackman, as rentmaker,
As bikebaron and brownbattler;
As Moorish sailor returning to Spain
In Afro-American frame;
As maker of songboy and songgirl.

Dear mirror:
Shining back might and moan
Shining back man and moon
Beating back song and saga
Ballrooming back blues and booze
Shingingback! Shiningback! Shiningblack!
Gibraltaric shoulder in a sandseepage;
Light-anchor in a nightmare's mouth;
Plougher/planter of seeds in the stomach of tomorrow.

Axe Song: Swordphone

for Julius Hemphill

HEAR:
Razorblades break and brocade air,
Hew wood and hack wind;
Hear sculptures of your mind . . .
Squeal or mutter some knife of speech of sound:
Give poise and drumcall to the air,
Bequeath breath a bolt of song: *riffin' riffin',*
Grind anger into genius,
Glean from wrath an order, a throne: *riffin' riffin',*
Sew threads of sounds
Through ancestral garments—
Needle, knife or handclap split
Natal cords and you blow babies into life:
Cutting to heal
Bleeding to seal: *riffin' riffin'*
            Blooding a muscle of notes,
            Hurling air-axes through stormwaters,
            Fishing for fireblades in an ocean of air.

Señor Pepe's Promenade

for Joe Gauthier, Sacramento, California

Food frets/promenades at *Señor Pepe's*
     Refried beans/
A goldenhostess in breastsmiles
Wearing restraining wall of knit
        /sweatered senorita/
Swelling up/out horizontal mountains
        /miniatured/
Burritos/
Enchiladas tucked in tortillas/
Mexicali beer
        /sun liquefied & bottled/
           and *sheGlows*
SheGlows, strung like flamenco melody
Rolling over the shores
        /slamming the beaches/
Of my ears;
From sunfractured frames/walls/
Mute as history and motionless as murals,
        /girldancers; sombrero'd senors stare/
Guarding this tradition
        /this hummingheat toil/
This KnifeForkPlate chatter and clatter,
        this feast and fiesta:
ChaCha-spiced lips
Smacking, wacking away at Mexican scrumptiousness;
"Wa-atch eet seen-yore, thee plate eeze hot,"
The waiter wises
        /from a blue vestjacket snaps/
Lowers baked dish to tablecloth
        /blue/

Straddling carpet
          /blue/
Whose designs/topo-rhymes scurry/wigglehurry like
tributaries
          /blue/   sky
And the room hatdances/
Drowning in Flamenco guitar
Glowing in Flamenco melody
Buttered in beangrease
          /and *sheGlows in* Mexicali Beer/

Songs From an Afro/Phone

for Darryl Redmond

Afro/phone
         Voice-in-a-veil/trumpet Gabriel-ing slavery's burial
Threading the needle's slit/
Taming the weather's spit;
Tiptoeing on a straightpin's roof
Through a soprano storm!
        /on an alto windblade/

Cymbals of lightning climbing clouds!
A bassly thunder strung in the land's groin!
The eye of the storm is a narrowhum/noddinghum,
The wipe of the wind a colossal laugh/flammable cough/;
As the footfalls of trillionth-trillionth man
Flail the drumbelly of the globe/
Flirt with a hum that is seasonal solemnity.

Afro/phone . . . tree-trumpet flouting/flaunting galaxial voices;
Cosmo horn and urn calling:
        Leaf-reed and lyrical!
        Reed-leaf and miracle!
Fantasy and finale of man forced/
Danced through wooden lips,
Through gravel jaws/
Across rivertongues/
Up from lakelarynx/
With mountainMagic churning stone to stereo coolness
In the hollow between these global titties
        between these global ditties:

That from the Afro/phone stream
That from the Afro/phone scream
That from the Afro/phone strike
Strum fire   /blasting the furnace of the sun/son

Swiftsong

for Isaac Hayes

A BluesBlindingSpeed!
    /BreakNeckBlackness!/
An ice-man
      /sun-sure/
Moaning;
A grouphood *gone-ing, lone-ing*, yeahhh!
A swordsong; a reedvoice;
Swift, *Jim!* swift and stiff:
Stiffer than stone, *blood,* and colder—*chilly-er!*
Gittin' up soulo . . .
Getting' down so-high . . .
My My My, Sister swiftJones, My My:
Pass the salad and the sisters, please!
Pass the pride/the buttered girl/gold!
Slap my hands into flapjack soul!
     hand/
        me/
           down/
              them/
                 blues
Rituals revolving at the speed of sound!
Swiftsong is a bloodclock called blues:
BreakNeckBlackness jammin' joy
     /jitterbugging the sun/
Gittin' up *soulo, Jim!*, being reel swift/
Stiff, slick with the grease/speed of the blues:
Jetdance, swift!
     IKE-kon/
        Swift!

Blues-Tone #1

for Sherman Fowler

From the ashnight of a *bluesfire*
I emerge a tune of history
A moon melody
A mood bar, a diminuendo spirit
Smoke-laureling and snorting *yestertorches* of wisdom/
Fireblades of wisdom on some beach
Bleached *Nth*-white:
> *"Flame-seed, Somewhere, Somehow!"*
As a tooltune of history
Cultivating/hoeing and harvesting
Little flames for larger fires
That I will bank to burnsongs
That I will sing to urn-sized loves:
> *"O fire-song, O seed, O need!"*
As a field of flame-seeds
Where ashes of a love-urn grow;
Flakes of passion under *bluefires*
Under *bluesfires* lipping the coat-tail,
The frayedhem of tomorrow: the *bluesglow*
The *blueglow*, the *blackglare* of desire,
Of wish and of wail:
> *"Fire-song, Bluestongs, Someday soon!"*

Blues-Tone #2

for Jerry Herman and Other Black Writers

Blues-tone/blues-drone on a typewriter:
    "Blue Rites! Blue Rites!"
Blue thumps of drumpen pleading/
Exhorting paper screens—
Rap-tap! drums of inundation, of syncopation
And a bodybeat/ an ideo-beep in ideophone/
A drivinghome, a drive-suite
Against the eternal mattress/the clay carpet
Of eternal rhythm/of divine rhyme
Flowing from feet/street
Into sacred fingers/
Fingers spilling folkhymns across a giant ellipsis
And crocheting riddles through crossworded weapons:
    "Blue Rites! Blue Rites!"
Fingers bledblue through penprayer
Through type-key cadence: churchchant and dogboogie—
Rap-tap! and centuries collide or speed by
Rap-tap! and ancestors swarm or sugar-thought the head
Rap-tap! and the type is a tear, making words sag
Rap-tap! and urge is an owl, staring from weewee words in the
    night;
Blue-tone on a typewriter: *Rap-tap!*
Breastplated, soul-insulated and bledblue;
Heartflamed fingers scratching, *RAP-TAP!*
Scraping the epidermis of the mind.

Stone Song

ROCKCHANT: clickclatterclash thoughts/ of need
Gourdgall/tallstories/fable-black
Sunstones, starstiff ageless dirt:
Whimpering before great *clockstone!*
         before great *metronome!*
        before great *time-gong!*
Marble-mind
Granite-gut
Boulder-strut
Sandcement-hut
Erection ROCK! high/noon/height
UpSOAR! phallic/fossil/song . . . rigidrhythm
Daddydrumthump: rock of ages!
         rock of gages!
         clock and cave, cage of mazes!
Interdependence—
Hardwater from solid-air /water frozen to stone/ transparent
    stone
And temperature *rock-a-bye-baby*
        Rock-a-my-soul in the bosom of Africa

Hardness, is the hardhum of change—
Hardness, the softsteel of love-rocks.

Natal Song

The outward landscape scars/ often
Scissors and sizzles/ the insides;
But beneath the tough-hide
Of race and selfpride,
We contain-the-pain
Quietfingering the refrain—
                /"Sandpaper rubbing my dream!"/

Growing withoutward and withupward
Yet withinward like erring chinhairs
To *self,* sunken sage of memory:
Those re-comings that tranquilize/
Sooth and sandpaper the mind.

The country in embryo *burns* in us;
Burns us, is scalding liquid
And redhot pokerlikelance;
This nation, nodding/gnashing, of the belly
Is drumhumhard; ulcer-knotted yet fist-coiled;
Is rockquarry in earth quickflesh.

Rockpeople, *treetrue,*
Carrying carcass and country:
No vain and *landlesssong.*

Big Sister Song

for Ethel Mae Redmond, 1928-1998

Helping us grow up-out-in guillotined/stillbore
Those jewel-laden years in the mind of darkdiamonds
That was/is you, solid-set and lightning-lit.

We, the younger-elders, knew-and-knew-not the source
            /even as we sought the sauce/
Of your corrugated concern, your candid care,
And of your vigils and visits by-bus, by-foot, by-laugh, by-tear.

And "Mae" came constantly, a sober sun, carting smiles
Fixed as forms/flexible as flames licked by cynical winds;
In cotton dresses, "May," carrying bags—bearing guessed-at-
        June joys:
Came clocklike with questions, with cautions:
Measles? Mumps? Books? Shoes? Kindling? Coal for the stove?

Littled lives, hop-scotching/patty-caking on love,
Sprouted/flung toward this grand sistermother, toward Black
Upstance, across lore, across land, across life—
To laugh and to lash—*to a song of branching, a song of
        sooning.*

Lone Song

First fears, first tears on autumn window pains,
Left over hurt from summer

/dregs of Illinois

madness/

California song is subtle sting;
California chill is quiet, coy—cat/walk—
Not noisy and nervous like midwestern winters.

My mood, then, often comes—is drumhummed—by mail;
My fury, my flame, my fidget caught postcard-quick,
Caught and cornered,
           /bulletinboarded/shored upon saltfilled tomorrows/

Brother Sister Nephew Niece:
Vital vibes on wire, on lyre—kincords/
Bloodcords of sounds or strings: spontaneous
COMBUSTION of blood inside *trees*, inside *seeds* and *shells*—
Inside xylophones, telephones and saxophones.

Love Song

In the madness, in the *madsting*
Of windherds grabbing
         /goring mud & dust/
At you in gallops
         /in gulps/
Or flameforests gathering you together
In coppergreen bundles of fire-grass
Or jetbreath collecting you in the arms
Of its lumberous storms,
In the *madsting* of hell-beheld,
I maintain my cool;
         Knowing that my promise, baby,
Is a mountain/is a sun of consistency
Is a doorknob of nature
Is a rainstorm of romance—
Here, then, this song:
Know my love, kinetic and corrugated;
Know this ocean of need, this fever of urgency;
Know this center that is quietchant,
Clumsy-Core,
Yet roar/distant and immediate/of *secret choruses*
         /Madsting! Madsting!/
Of vital forces.

Itch-Song
The Black lawyer seen as warrior at the bench

for Jimmy Long, Sacramento

Itch-hour,
Itch hour in a courtroom warm with worry:
Where justice sometimes is courtjester/
Joker in a stacked deck;
Itch-hour, also, in a street-world,
Bitching-hour where truth is a color-couched nightmare:
>   *"Let my people Go!"*
Itch-hour for steel-tongue warrior
Whose color is *handcuffs,* is *straitjacket,* is *cage*
From whose clutches he must stage trial,
Stage trial and community triumph:
>   *"Let my people Go!"*
Bitching and stitching hour, bewitching hour,
For warrior! wishbringer! oracle! mojoMan!
Prophet of the larynx!
Peerless priest! Black pontiff in exile!
Wordwick and *wordspear;*
Itch-hour, again, and the ghetto gonggong is silent;
Silent in this place/in this joustroom
Where Blackmen caucus iridescent mouthmagic
To juju judges and jaw-frozen jurors:
Itching hour where mothers kneel or nod
And white bondsmen bargain;
Where hums flockfather and swordsworn troubador;
Caller, grandseer, summoner, sage and medicine-man:
Nat Turner, sunglassed, at the moaning bench;
Malcolm at the pearly gates;
Stokely stroking the River Jordan;
King, shoulderholstered, at the mountaintop:
>   *"Let my people Go!"*
Bookbrawn/based, lathered in blood, folk-supple
And songborne: folkseam and folksun:
>   *"Let my people Go!"*

Trek-Song, Mack-Song

for James Baldwin, Ralph Ellison, and John Steinbeck

Grapes of wrath, ground/danced into wine:
      /"Drink wine, spodie-yodie, drink wine!"/
Georgia-pine-high, America's *invisible man*
Stammers or performs stunts
In the country's viscera . . .
Is flushed through the anals
Of the national debt:
      /"Drink wine, whale with them plucks!"/
Trekking, trekking, trucking:
Hauling ass, marijuana, cocaine,
Hashish, heroin, LSD and much dick;
Trekking through Memphis, St. Louis, East Boogie,
MoTown, Cleveland, Philly, The Big Apple,
New Ark — — — — —
Macking across the Mohave Desert,
Riding thin rivers into Orange County, California,
Watutsi-ing through Watts and Compton;
Trucking */"Express yo'self: in a hurry!"/*
Trekking, Macking on a conveyor belt moving to the rear:
      /"Drink wine, my man"/
Whaling, smoking, cooking, bucking, snorting:
      /"Don't let the man make you turn no tricks, Jim!"
Runsong, beat-up-and-done song;
Ever-winning/ever-losing/ever-ebbing trektune.

Steelsong in Stillwater

for The Four Tops and "Smokey" Bill Robinson

The penis of thought *upthrusts,*
Erects columns we must climb
To peer/prevail/above oppressive
Urine that *drowns* our gods
And *dams* our nostrils;
Downthrusts, sunray-steady,
To dagger deceptive surface waves . . .
To drill eye and mind into *yesterhorizons*
In stillest depth, with stoniest stare,
With sharpest song:
       "Deep river . . . my home is over Jordan"
To that level where water becomes lead stance,
Becomes stoic river of blues, becomes even sharper song,
Becomes ancestral gong steelsounding/stillpounding;
Thrusts to inject bloodjuices into deep heart of thought,
Steep backbone/spine-ladder of folkdreams, veins
Of visions and leathery feet of pilgrimage:
       "Deep river . . . my home is over Jordan"
Leathery feat of legend-building, leathery feet of lore;
Thrusts a remedy, Thrusts a melody, Thrusts a male-note:
       "Steel Waters Run Deep!"

Miles Song

for Miles Davis

Goldlipped blunderbuss,
Diamoned eyed derringer,
Cool air carver and fashionfreak:
Moonsong and moonson.

Moonsongster and lunarlyricist for a nightfaced nation,
Croonbearer shuttling a blue cord,
Polyscreaming his hex-songs,
Refingering a three-keyed note-fryer:
Blowing soundbeams and phonic rainbows;
Hissing/sighing/humming through the sun:
Root-tooting and root-toting;
A totem of tones and tidal walls:
      Miles from home
      Miles to roam
(*Clifford Brown* reincarnated in the subconscious chorus
Of this goldlipped windfencer: *Clifford*)
*Yard*song, foot- and inch-song: *Miles from home;*
Miles, multitudes, whole storms crushed to soundgraphs,
Fed through an Afro-phone: darksong in coppermoon.
      Miles to roam
      Miles to moan
Cotton-lipped flute, note sizzler, brassblare and brassbone:
      Riffin'!
      Riffin'!
      Riffin'!
Blood boiling upto air-stream upto Afro-urn,
Condensing to acoustigraphs,
Steady, yet startling as fixed stares/echoes caught in stone
      pots.

Hummin', Hookin' & Cookin'

for Sam and Dave

You got me hummin'

Bodies bloat the air
        /into an after-supper casserole/
Bodies sing /now/ and are *lovinglybruised,* brushed,
           Plaitted and pig-tailed
           On a shifting bed of coals;
Caringly battered and cured,
           Marinated in perfume, talcum powder
           /after-shave love/
Sauced, ensouled,
Saladed in unintelligible vowels
           colliding consonants/
In whispers, in hums, in hisses
           /through the bodies' alleys/
Through the sensuously uttering utensils/utonsils
           /baking and broiling/
In sweat, in tongue-tickling jawjuice;
Cookin' in pillow-cased ovens of ecstasy,
           /on sheet-covered thrill-grills/
Hookin' the meals of fulfeelment
Onto clothes-pin fingers,
Fingers that grip medium-rare rumps
Or welldone joypebbles glistening
On shores of liver-like skinskillets:
           /*succulent* and *surrealuscious!*
Peppery parting of a vaginal menu—
Hocks *hummin'* in fried sweat,
Boiling in sweat:
Need enunciated in beerflavored barbecue;

Body-cuisine scrumptiously offered:
      /fillet of desire/   /soufflé/
Stewed orgasms, groundbeef,
        /milkwarm tongues on platters/
Fingerforks peeling back the fore-skin
Of brownbananas:
      Bodies marinated, *lovingly bruised,*
Fried in sweat, in spit,
      /lovingly bruised/
Talcum powder on medium rare muscles,
      Lips sippin' lips,
Bodies marinated:
      /hummin'/
         /hookin'/
            /cookin'/

Lyrics and Lines of Blood from
a Black Painting

Here and there and here
                   /you see/
Is a painting—
Colorbothered and brooding blackly:
        My song!
        Your song!
        Our song!
A mirror, mood blue, around us, surrounding us
               /a lovelake splashing/
Splashing back waves and selves
               /back selfwaves/
        Waking us with stare-dances:
        Waving at us—
        Warning us—
        Washing us of all artificiality—
        Purifying out blood—
        Clarifying our windlore—
Locked in trees,
Lured to riverbottoms,
Laden with *amens* and *omens*
               /with old men/
Blackbeauty naked,
Gnarled /sometimes/ like knuckles
Of the recently lynched—
        My face!
        Your face!
        Our faces!
Now the map, the rap that becomes a tune
               /tap-tap-tap/
Cartography in the palm, in the applause!
        Yeah, like *bad* man
        Yeah, like *bossBad* man

        Yeah, like a *bad-dad* man

I mean STRENGTH/mean STEEL;
Yeah, talking 'bout iron *TEARDROPS!*
Wow, like metal THOUGHTS:
>   *The Rocks of Ages!*
>   *We Rock the ages!*
We/here (there-here: hear! Can you hear?) are a painting
>   /mood colors/ /multicolors/
Flowers! Flowers!
Growing in gardens of air—
>   /flames fidgeting on clouds/
Above clouds—
PIONEERS pivoting on the sun;
PIONEERS pivoting on the sun:
>   John Henry is the sun—
>   Can you *dig* it?
>   John Henry is the man—
>   Can you *get* to that?
Oh yeah! He's the ONE! He's the ONE! He's the ONE!
>   /You're the ONE/
>   /I'm the ONE/
>   /He's the ONE/
>   /She's the ONE/
>   /We're the ONE/
Can you *get* to that!
Can you *get* to that!
Can I *get* a witness!
If so, then RUN!
>   Now RUN!
>   RUN on!
>   Now RUN!
>   RUN on!
>   NOW . . . RUN AND TELL THAT!

Note: Curtain speech from the script *The Night John Henry Was Born*:
A Black Folk Saga, produced, directed and partially written by EBR at
Southern University, Baton Rouge, Louisiana, during summer of 1972.

Cane-Brake-Blues

Remembering Jean Toomer's Cane

Got me some canebrake blues/baby/this sugarpain sho is bad;
Got me some canebrake blues/baby/this sugarpain sho is bad;
This sweet/sweet sore /man/ just keeps me happy-sad.

Cane blade cuts my mind / make my thoughts runred;
Cane blade cuts my mind / make my thoughts runred;
Cane dagger in my brain / knife-sweetenin' my head.

Cane crams wind down my throat
        /I'm hollerin from earth's hole;
Cane crams wind down my throat
        /I'm hollerin from earth's hole;
Sounds just symphonizing / resurrecting my old, old soul.

Got some canebrake blues, sweet/mama,
Got some canbrake blues
Got some canbrake blues, sweet/mama,
        /got some canebrake blues/
But with this sugarpain power
How can I lose
How can I lose
How can I lose . . .

Railroadrhyme

Remembering East St. Louis (& Rush City)

Specs of light
> /looming lunging/
Growing out of roundhouses,
Exploding as nightsuns
And streaking through a blues-silent dark;
> /moon-stalked night/
Underneath rails, below tracks,
> /"tracks of my tears"/
Underside asphalt scar/tear or carpet
> /the hellside/
Co-flows the blood of tree-roots
And BlackWorkCrews:
> *"We built the roads*
> *And towed the loads!"*
Beneath rails   /the fingers/
BurntFleshBlack lie fossil-like
Waiting passage of trial and train
Or wound-opening refrain:
> *"We built the roads*
> *And towed the loads!"*
Calls and cries   /now/   trapped
> /casketed/
In the rhyme of the line:
Mo Pac, BM & O, Illinois Central,
Midnight Special: "Bringggg Myyy Bloodback!"
As the rib-rubbing, steel-nubbing engine
Grunts/grinds past macktown/past shack town:
> *"We built the roads*
> *And towed the loads!"*

Sharpeville Sting/Song

for Oliver Jackson, Painter
After "Sharpeville Series"

Mechanical sharpshooters
       /villains/
Reload lightning sticks
That mutter/sputter harsh sparklanguage
At hungryflesh huddled in the streets;
Sharpeville Song, Sharpeville Symphony
Harpoons through bodies, slaughter-house bunched,
Sagging from blood-dirt dampness,
Lagging behind life   /given up to lore/
To folkgossip and handlers of decaying human décor.

Sharpshooters singing /now/ from pompous books:
Word-barrages /automatic elocutionists
       /sugarfill the fleshholes;
Journalists and Jurists trotting
/In high-breed grace/ across conscience courts,
Pantomiming gods/ghouls and meandering in mouthwash.

Sharpeville knowing /now/ that ancestral bowmen
Will blow-dart a deed-for-deed vengeance;
That underneath trees juju-ers sing sharpwrath:
As Sharpevillains chop at natal cords
       /try to brake birthing nationhood/
With swords of technology /mindless slashes/
With knives of false knowledge:
Sharpeville sting rings in earthbelly
For BlackJustice; for redemption of
Unprovoked suffering, of *UnAskedFor* death.

Sonnet Serenade/Soulo Beauty

for Gwendolyn Brooks

Behold! the forms and rhythms of my face:
Choral trees and soulos limbly bowing;
Greenhiss/grasslow and moanful in sparkspace,
Caught crying/caroling and know-howing;
Sometimes in gusty *soulsoliloquys*
Within vastvalleys and mountainous songs;
Or much/iterated with ah's and me's,
Short/circuited or shattered against gongs.

A lord-length voice invades these jungle sparks:
Neoning/drumscripting a passion-rain
Which seeds tear-tunes and in the drumpath marks:
A cool/mellow maid of song and a main
Squeeze close-held in sound-arms, in hip song-rap;
Whose love, buttoned in gold, is your lyre-lap.

Mood-Afro/Fire

Thinking of "Duke" and "Mood Indigo"

From a spiritual quiver
Soars an ache/ an arrow;
Comes steel spines, holy hypodermics, rich marrows;
Comes boiling boneJuice we drink
        /fluid-triggered thoughts/
BoneJuice we inject into trees for safe-keeping;
/Mood Afro/ keepsakes trance-clasped in trees/
Knuckle-rooted in *jewelrock,* in fatherground;
Dance-dark clefs cuddled/huddled
Readied in bowstring across hearth, across heart,
Unleashed in rhymes of time, of tart:
        of *Elegance!*
        of *Poetrees!*
        of *DanceBodies!*
        of Bloodstones!
        of *Jewelrock!*
When the neck is nailstiff
With the virus of oppression,
With the virus of mis-history:
Mood Indigo is a cadence-test of fire,
Of *BluesFlame*: Mood Afro,
The midwife of the moon,
Blackblanket and electric quilt
Close-circuiting a furled world,
Circling a world with quiver
        /spirit current/
A shiver of harmony, of bone/hardharmony:
        of *ElegantPoetrees!*
        of *DanceBodies in Bloodstones!*
        of *Jewelrock!*

Happenin' Harmony

for Marvin Gaye, Curtis Mayfield & Margaret Walker

We are voice-lifted people/
/elevators humming suns/
Syncopating profound noise: people of . . .
/Garrulous pride/
Purple grace
". . . bloody peace . . ."/
Quiet moonmurmuring devotion;
Blackbalanced soilfooted
/darker than pre-creation hollowness/
Lighter than the WORD,
Faithfull as fertility symbols/silent temptresses
In ageless voice-tapestries: *and ancienter!*
Africanbones bledred through treebark arms.

"Moving on up!" a starphonic scale
/and across HOW MANY rivers!/
Along roadblades and knife-notes,
Moving to the bluesgloom of God,
The bluesgroom of a *Lady Day Like Goddess;*
The people of knuckle-wrought calm;
Of dimple-clad, riddle-bad, melodies;
Of intonated ecstasy:
"What's happenin', brother?"
The people yesterspirits serenade
With parables/preachments transported
In the wombvoice of the wind:
"What's happenin', brother?"
"What's happenin', sister?"

Southern Sound:
A Brooding Under Blood

for Melvin Butler, Pinkie Gordon Lane & Charles Rowell
after summers, 1971-1972, Baton Rouge, Louisiana

Creole, collard greens
And hoodoo hymns against a gumbo sky—
> *"Soil song*
> *Spoil song"*
Dixie chant is Black road to *steelhammermountain*
DeepSouth ritual is discreet strength,
Darklore is harpdance in a lyricfield—
> *"Spoil song*
> *Soil song"*
Fatback, hogjowls and juju
And the mind is farmland/is swarmland
For this newnation in embryo,
For this bee-busy commotion
And earthward polychatter—
> *"Soil song*
> *Spoil song"*
Bloodland, blooddocks and bloodfruit
And a child, ripe;
And a mind, ripe: ripe with sting or strut
Like sugarblades of cane
Or Louisiana browngirls whose passions
Gestate in volcanos,
Hesitate under quiet cotton colors—
> *"Spoil song*
> *Soil song"*
Dixie Chorus is an African call/
Watusi-tall, *greening with upsongs*
Hoodoo hymns in a lyricfield
Against a gumbo sky.

Dance Bodies #1

Spitfire! from *BlackFleshMotors*
/whirhums/
Under acrobatic howls:
Zig-grip! Zig-grip! Zig-grip!
Zag-lore! and bodies brush air;
Dip-twist! Down-bend! Dip-twist!
And kissing palms pancake/applaud air,
Chop smoke/humpscreams:
JamesBrowning the breakdown!
BrakeDowning the JamesBrown!
Washing air with sugarsweat/
With antiseptic potion and polish;
Caroling *fleshmotors* flinging/
Ringing from shirt or skirt:
                "Boogaloo on through!
                  Breakdown the walls, brother!
                  Boogaloo on through!"
Footfire on floor of hot coals:
Split! Get up!! Toe-turn!
                /Split!/   /Toe-turn!/
Heel-tunes screeching:
                "Bank-here! Break-there!"
Kissing palms pancake/paralyze the air:
Sugarsweat sterilizing air
With gymnastisc intelligence/
With brain dance acrobatics/
With spitfire from *fleshmotors*— humming:
                "Boogaloo on through!
                  Breakdown the walls, brother!
                  Boogaloo on through!"

Think-Tune

for The Impressions

Beneath the bite/
Beneath even the night of life
Thumps a chorus of thought-keys—
Brainlites/rites burning quiet songs of paradox,
Lyrics of unheaval, into smug limousines of flesh;
Into robot bones produced/packaged by Colonizers Ltd.

Beneath the ire   /the wire/   of confinement
Beneath even bargain-store attire and status,
Elevators shuttle woe'd souls to penthouse/
Alley rhythms;
To shotgun shacks or highriseriots of the mind
Where blood thinks thicker than life,
Flowsfaster than water,
Runs/slower than bullets;
Where blood oils keyboards of brains
Playing rainbow ballads;
Playing *pride* with cerebralsplendor;
Playing grindbump/
                a deathlife hump/
                quick quick quickened on a guitar tongue/
                quiet songs of paradox, mellow messages/
                ambiguous carpets of sounds/
                    coolriots-of-the-mind.

Lyrics for Leon

for "Homeboy" Leon Thomas and "Spirits Known and Unknown"

> *songstitch to mend*
> *songstitch to mend*

Encoding a cry, a call, a blues-epic
> /turning song into corduroy sky/

You birth a feathery voice/scream!
Airborne in ridges of an African overcast:
Brick-throated balladeer!
Decoding hieroglyphics in the groin,
In the script of ancient drumvoices—
> *songstitch to mend*
> *songstitch to mend*

"Leaping Leon": erupting into rhapsodic mountains:
> *"oola-boo oola-boo oola-boo*
> *oola-boo oola-boo oola-boo*
> *oola-oola oola-oola oola-oola*
> *oodle-ee boo-ee oodle-ee boo-ee*
> *oodle-la-boo oodle-la-boo"*

Torchnotes! Flame-throat!
Raging in phonic forests
> /tree-tunes/

In fireblades that chop and copper-crust
The corduroy sky of song—
> *songstitch to mend*
> *songstitch to mend*

Soulo- and echo-child, seedspring of sound
Eloping, groping,
With demons of coastal storms/
Noiseless mistresses of docks and deserts:
Riverrhythm, exorcising *spirits known and unknown,*
Moving up/down ladders of sunstreams;
Chorusing/caressing stars, making tones galactic,
Orchestrating initial buzzes and hums:
> *songstitch to mend*
> *songstitch to mend*

Tune for a Teenage Niece

for Jeanine Spencer

Smile/rippling river of dance—
Flow, blow green soul-lyre
Ballooning under brown flesh:
Song/swirl, startling as claps
Of unexpected waves;
Girlriver dancing its drumdeep past,
Its boogalooborn/e day,
Fluteflown afro freight
*Grand*mother/mama/aunt—sun-led—
Yesterwhistling confluence
       /childwoman and charmsong:
        "Brown blues and honey-river, girl!
         Blues-brown and river-honey, girl!
         Girlmother gonna sing her song someday, boy!
         Brown blues and honey-river, girl!
Smile/river dancing, splashing flame-waves
Applaud and burn/mold *brownfruit,*
Afro-plum,
River symphony, water ritual:
        "Brown blues and honey-river, girl!
Girlriver, spiced as pot liquor, flowing up/under
From queenmother's heartbeam; from magic and marmalade;
Fluteflown to fleshdance and birdgrace:
Flowing to *omen,* to *woman:*
        "Brown blues and honey-river, girl!"

Sound of a Heart-Train

for John Coltrane & Johnny Hartman
(Impulse Stereo LP: -40)

Twice/together:
Two rails of ache hurtle this groupheart
Rails—ailings—of sound moaning, honing stone paths
       /Stone lone/
Bleeding and balladeering a dignity of stresses;
Tracks criss-crossing a scale of time and tones;
Making *fancydance* the ear
       polylayered the movement, *the lyric:*
       lumbersome *the love;*

Beneath rails, between rails
Daring drumheart arches a crescendo of thumps and thunder,
Bumps and hums: a cardiacting rhythm section,
Drumbass, for rails of sound, for ails of sound,
Soaring! Exploring!
       Horned voice!
       Brassflesh and rail!
       Cocaine, sometimes, and tail!
Powdered blood blown/thickened to stone
To tracks of steelrhyme:
Shuttling invisible cargo, indivisible cargo,
The *weight,* the *worry,* the *freight,* the *fret,*
The goldenstool of stereo tucked in/under
In/under rails of ache hurtling this groupheart:
       Horned voice!
       Brassflesh and rail!
       Cocaine, sometimes, and tail!

After a While/Wail

for Marinda Vestal

After a while/
The sea sucks itself into an unconscious crawl,
    Caterpillaring back/forth
Between its pits and its peaks/
    Waving to gigantic cottonballs
Blotting/bloating the sky,
    Rubbing and polishing the naked shore
With its salty stomach.

AFTER A WHILE/
    The sea is a somnambulist
Humrunning/ a belching bloodshot eye/
    Flowstalking the mudflesh face
    /the rollrhyme of earth's TwentyFourHourTwist/
Barbecuing on an axis before the great/grill
    /sun/

After a while/
    The sea is a source,
A lugging song of yesterblood/
Or a leaping taunt to an hypnotic moon
Whose gravity /whose depravity/
Concerns the sea: *after a while.*

After a while/
    /all the while/
/anywhile/
    The sea scans us   /again/
Tolls our tasks   /and waits/
And we are *upthrown* to shore
By the sea's gaze which
    /after a while/
Takes us
    /takes all/

In the Fleshflame that is Her Face

In the fleshflame that is her face,
The fire burns her clearer to me;
And in her apricot ears, the stereophonic
Flames lick and crack, playing playing
Back the sounds of teeth roasting in gumgrease.

In the fleshflame that is her face,
The nose is an anvil of leavening:
A symmetrical center, a symmetrical song
Of two hollows bleeding the air with
Their silent drum-operas.

In the fleshflame of her face
Lie launch pads for eye-rockets,
Two springboards of sight stalking
And reaching the rims of things—
For eyes reach further than arms.

Oh flameflares that are her eyes!
Oh fireflies that are her eyes!

In the fleshflame of her face
Old urges and urns burn: Plenipotentiary
Pyres of the past watching over
This charred-copper queen:

The flash/flame that is her face,
The force that is her fire,
The flame that is her fight,
The fuse that is her light,
Is the fleshflame of her face!

Drumfeet on the Soil

*DRUMFEET ON THE SOIL, ON THE SANDROADS OF
    THE MIND!*

FLESH-PISTONS PRANCING, THE EARTH'S ENGINE!

*IT IS A COMING FORTH, THE NIGHT WITHIN US
    COMING FORTH/COMING FORTH!*

THE NIGHT WITHIN US IS COMING FORTH!

*FEET BEATING, BEATING, BEATING SEEDS INTO
    THE SOIL!*

FEET BEATING SOIL!
FEET BEATING SOIL!
FEET BEATING SOIL INTO SEED INTO SOIL!

THE NIGHT WITHIN US IS COMING FORTH!
COMING FORTH!
COMINGFORTH!

Note: Choral introduction of dancers during one sequel of the ritual *River of Bones*, produced, directed and partially written by the author for audiences at California State University, Sacramento; and Southern University, Baton Rouge, Louisiana, 1970-71.

SECTION SIX
In a Time of Rain & Desire
Early 1970s

EBR Reading in Sacramento, California. 1974.

Boyjewel: Dazzle-Man

for Godson Ross Mark Williams,
Born April 12, 1973 at 8:15 AM

New Blink in the world—
Coiled fleshsong, *Mark*ing time,
In the crib of caress—
On the incline of love:
   Hey hey boybloom!
   Hey hey manflower!
   Hey hey songbud!
Nightsong, spice-wind in the world—
Blues coil, fleshknot, on the tree of man,
In the sun's constant veil—
In the high hovel of special grace:
   Hey hey boybloom!
   Hey hey mandance!
Manfret unfurling toward every-which-away—
Manseed, planting muscles in Chicago-ground:
   Hey hey boybloom!
   Hey hey manbud!
   Hey hey tree-tune!
Swirlcry, acrobat in coil, blinking prince—
Totemic majesty, *watch watch watch* the world open!:
Watch watch watch, dig!, the world open!
But stretch but coil but sing but watch!
   Hey hey boytree!
   Hey hey Afro-fidget!
   Hey hey boybloom!
   Hey hey!
   Hey hey!
   Hey hey!

Main Man Blues

Do you know my
Slap-a-hand, lend-a-hand main man?

Dirt-deep podner,
Quick-reeling, nigger-feeling friend, then?

Knife-blocker,
Vagina stopper,
Wit-knitted—not-to-be-shitted—bad man?

Have you ever had the *main man blues?*
Have you ever re-dug or coat-tailed
That cleanfully nasty harbinger of corner cuss?

Brothergone/Brother-coming?
Spitfire well digger
Who never got no bigger?
That ghetto-phonic nigger?

In the streets, on the sheets—where we sopped up our own
   blood;
In the churches—where we prayed, preyed, squinting
At fat old sisters or plumb-luscious classmates?

Brothergone/Brother-coming?
Hot rags macker, righteous!
Hot cock tracker, righteous!
Bigdaddy, uncle of mercy in the git-down times:
Slap-a-hand, lend-a-hand, main man?

Postscript

At 2 am this morning
          I awoke
2 am webbed in a wrinkled geography of sheets
          I awoke
To see your hands ploughing your hair
Your body an incompleted *S*
In fetus-like tranquility,
Cocooned in the port of your last orgasm;

With throttle open, I thought,
          You always swell so-quickly
          And I grow to contain, refrain you:
          Yet, like a tree, you branch and branch
          In the forest of my multiplying hungers.

At 2 am your rage is a timid whir: otherwise, othering:
And I wonder, What voodoo vassal shrank you so?
What manner of God forested your fruits and,
At 2 am, shrinks and calms your fire into the crook of my arm?

Not Rejection:
But Complex and Painful Truth

I cannot solve the riddle of your needs
Nor salve the cerebral pricking of your pain;

You cannot solve the silence of my chill
Nor what you see as sadism in my thrill
    /the strange night-air passing between us/
/shuddering our bodies & shifting our allegiances/
You say I owe you the luxury of a lie
    /that I should stay!/
You say worry is the flipside of ecstasy
I say worry is the midwife of life
    /O decisions!/
And through the same door love enters and exits
And through the same door passes game and blame
    /O decisions!/
But love is not a baton in a relay race:
Neither a nugget nor a broach
    /And how can I return what I never received?/
And if I could give you dividends on your love
How could I repay God for breath?
    /O decisions!/
And chances;
I take chances in the whirlwind
    /in the laundromats of change/
On the washingboards of life—
To be give-less is not rejection
But complex and painful truth.

Heart-Wounds Do Not Heal

For asylum from such wounds
There is always a scab:
        /some mascara/
Sunglasses for flooding wells in the face
        /laughter/
Withdrawalism or anonymous liquids in a glass
        /humor/
Laces or silks or high-hats
        /excuses/
A new surge: a new risk: a new squeeze
        /vanity/
An analysis, a tear-length night, resoluteness
        /indulgence/
Long sleeves for clawed flesh, for itch-marks
        /wherewithal/
And night dawns a mirror of daylight
On the immediacy of the mind
        /worry/
And, again, the reflection is actual
        /a sigh refracted in screams/
        /and a ballistics test says the tears came from blood/
Where the bed is a cage in which to wrestle with night
Or be still and listen to the gasping of the dark
Or the heart *wounded and wounded and wounded*
Which will not *heal*
And the ghosts you cannot kill!

Miss Teenage Black Sacramento

20 May 73: Woodlake Inn

Embryonic elegance—

Ancestrail echoes
In the falsetto fricatives
Of the Mellophonics—

Love sprinkles the boardwalk—

Gleaming mommas & daddies—

Love is a young woman—
    Girlflowering,
Dressed in suns and sundowns,
Glowing into the *befores* */gleeing/*
And the *far evers*—

Love as Upbringing

Remembering Gilbert Easterly and Rush City

Where the willows drag the ground
And coal sheds
Slant tar-paper heads
Toward ring-wormed sunflower stalks,
My love grew
From a seed
Draped in a tear poised in grand/mother's eye—
In East St. Louis,
In the saintlessness of slot-machines
In the ring of gunfire
In the cackle of hussies
In beneath-the-bridge taverns
My boyhood notions
Were nudged, made adventurous,
By the pipe-puckered/snuff-stained
Lips of teethless troubadors—
Strumming/strumming
Out their blemishes and boasts
On gatemouth guitars and widowed washing boards—
In the *southend* chorused by the roar of trains
Rushing through Rush City:
A crater,
A scowl of agony—and a heavenly hamlet—
On the face of a land
Saddled by the bridges of whitemen:
Whose tracks   /screeching & screeching/
Were long-play records fused from the fossils of Blackmen and
Redmen.

O the melody of freight and rails!
In Beulahland
Where the dead died, often, at home
And coffins lay open
In doily-decorated living rooms:
My hunger for chainless manhood upsoared!
In the shacks of my mind
In the visions of cotton dresses
In tattered totems of hope
Of a grandwise grandmother
My love grew from blisters
My love grew from sore rumps
My love outlined against the gutter-grim sunken streets
Against geniuses nodding
In unlabeled bottles.

Underneath Africa

Underneath Africa crawl the fisty roots
Of black, brown or beige fleshtrees
That cross *middle passages* ntu Arkansippi
   where dried blood swirls
        /or stands staunchly/
Shining in its baobab-brilliance like Benin bronze.
In extended family forests,
Love lopes or sprints in
Dances of harvest or hunt or death
While struggle-gnarled hands
Luxuriate in quilted, kitchen and doily'd delicacies.

I Can Never Unlove You

To *not want*
Is to *not exist*
Is to be de-minded
Is to be disembodied
Is to be disem-personed
And float like an apparition
Into the non-where
Into the gray whim of limbo
And that is why I can never unlove you:
        why I can never dismantle my passion
        why I can never decompose my desire

To reel in my cautious need
Is to be unclumsy in hyperposture
Is to be a cursed garden, growthless
Is to be made breathless by outside strictures
And nod in noon-sun like
A drunken lizard—
A slitherless drip on the echo of love
        on the back of some nomadic breeze
        on the coattail of sanity
And that is why I can never unlove you
        why I can never unnotice the flames you forge
        why I can never unloose my eyes from their aim

I can never unlove you
Though I can re-love you before another moon
I can never un-need you
Though I can re-grieve the night-stained caresses
I can never not want you
Though I can re-cry the ancientest ocean:
I can never unlove you:
Unlove you . . .
Never.

Midway in the Night: Blackman

Blackman
    /midway in the night/
In the Beaulahland of cabarets
      /bronco-busing the moon/
Silent is the howl, hung & mouth-held—
Your penis wrapped, rope-like,
'Round your neck:
Your penis clotted, knot-like,
At your throat:

Your manhood dog-loosed
On the auction block
Of an American whim:
Your love cluttered with white fear
Your womanview hazed by the rat-tat-tat
Of assassins who snipe your future
And ambush your history:
Black man,
Lover man:
Man of much-dick
Night-fuck hero
Quick-fire artist
Dashman—
Don't let your penis protrude, goat-horn-like,
Through your skull
Butting its way through
The tender muscular enclosures of your woman:
So anxious you cannot take the last shirt
Off the back of your mind:
So driven you cannot
Utter, in low register / in timed-tone,
The special name of your love.

Night Love: Postscript

Dry rings of love. Lull.
Sheets rippled rolled. Ridges. Horizons of the bed.
          /stillwaves of cloth/
Your legs listless plows. Bone-fled flesh.
In a fleshgarden
Orgasms grow. Sensual insignia.
Music. Night search. Liquid neon
Morning. Chill vault quiver.
First yawn of day.
Trees shudder. Showers for the mat of dawn.
Sun blinks. Sun bleats.
Dry rings of love. Love is a bedwetter.
Saliva on your thighs: Damballah's inscription.
Lust of last night: nude-scrawled bed-rings.
Hissdrone of shower. Bathroom giggle, gurgle.
Marvin Gaye's moan: *"Trouble Man" Trouble.*
Trouble:
          /*nobody* knows de trubble I see . . . /
Sun tears. Shower hissdrone. Your
Thighs cry: cringe from the sun's hexing eye.
Night shrinks back into your woods.
Shrinks back into the womb of God.

A Candle of Struggle Lights the Road

Around me
    /within me/
The greatest love / "no greater love"/
Flourishes & frets:
This struggle is a sharp
Point on the dial of my momentum
      /sharp point/
      —that jabs away at my
Intestinal freedomtude
Where oppression is a reality,
Blunt as a dream:
Around me
      /within me/
My brethren boil
And are cooked in open ovens of humiliation
Or pierced by needle-point
Or jailed by iridescent stripes & weaves
Or silenced by remute control of tv—
In me
      /around me/
The candle of struggle scorches the road
And burns for me; burns me:
Consumes me, sometimes,
In petite objectives
      And my people on the stilts of materialism!
      And my brothers doing about-faces
      Before natural gods—
It is a love weighty & war-lured
A come-late
A rise-early pain

Where a circle of boasts
Where a circle of threats
Cloaks the obsolescence of freedom fighters
Cloaks the desperation of daddies:
Where poets move moorless & craftless
To the temporary stars of prefabricated thrones
                /false thrones for false poets/
To love in all the clutter, Lord?
To love in all the clutter?

And the struggle is a constant cross:
Humming injustice against thorns unseen;
And color is my strength
And color is my nation
And color is an albatross around the ghetto's neck!

The greatest love flourishes, frets
My struggle/
And always always there is the sweet
Suburban urge to landscape the secret tears:
To paper the walls of agony with greenbacks:
To hurtle through my people's mire
In block-long pimpmobiles:
                /o temptation o temptation!/
Frothing love: this struggle a siren
Announcing that my guts have turned
To leather for the longfight:
Announcing that love is ambivalent armor:
A sword to fight with . . .
Or fall on.

I Know the Stigma

I know the stigma
        /attached to the guitar between my legs/
That sucks the Blackman
Into the driftwood of nonchalance
Where love is a lump in his throat
Where love is a tear
Forming premature stains in his eyes—
The stigma that seduces his manhood
And sets him sail
On jealous waters of America's fantasy
The stigma impaled on his penis
        /o bronze muscle/
And jutting through the tempestuous
Nights of American dreams:
Jutting—as charismatic skyscraper
That whitemen ponder
And whitewomen cuddle:
A spermato-seed in the garden of European mythos.

I know the opulence of white wombs
Into which the Blackman's mind
Sometimes falls—
I know the stigma of the vaginal cage
Where freedom writhes in eternal fetus
Where the embryo of Blacklove
Shrinks from the light of grownup needs.

I know the power of the fetish that dangles
Or coils between my legs
And hisses uncomfortably outside stud factories
I know the sub-gods of my body
And the lore-ladened jewels
That are not the heirlooms of America:

I know the stigmas
        Even as Africa sees/oozes through me
        Even as my woman waits in the night
The stigmas that cauterize my care
The stigmas my father shrank from
The stigmas that taunt/tame America
The colossus I must fight
Lest I remain a nomad
On the endless body of the Black woman.

Inside My Perimeter

Inside my perimeter
Of fears
A unit of guerillas
Strikes at the barbed-wire
Hovels that hoard our love
And incarcerate our needs.
Then an insurgent army
Storms the bastille of pride,
Shells this façade of custom,
Knells the collapse
Of the straw men inside us—
Accepts the sun,
Allows the contorted face of
Stress to smile again—
To glow again!
Allows Love to Live.

Rain Desire Rain Desire

Rain, desire
Desire, rain—
Joy-waters rise,
Fall;

Joy-waters leap,
Clap hands, roar through our abundance:
And the sky drips a sonorous tear
To my body contorted between your pillars
          /golden pillars/
My body weeping upon hilly thighs
And the fleshdoor of your lyrical corridor
Salved by sweat, by blood:
By rain
By desire
And I exit through a dawn that blares the chatter
Of artificial mornings; that drops a drape
Of light over the world's window
              over the dark torches we bear
              over our limb-lore
And the night rides an elevator
From the oasis of our ecstasies to the storehouse
Of remembrance: of relish:
Where rain hammers out memory
And the ghost of desire
Slips through wet thoughts:
Tiptoes on the damp dots of anxiousness:
                    of shiny climaxes.

Request (If It's Not Asking Too Much)

Long for me,
Baby,
Anchor me deep within
Your within,
Lodge my presence between
Your thoughts,
Let me alternate with your
Breathing,
Discriminate in my favor,
Labor late in my cause,
Go through changes with me!
Fashion your heart into a pen
Dipped in your blood and bleach/brand
My name into the sky,
Rise rise up against those
Who put bad mouth on me!

Stand stand Mama!
Stand still
And wait relentlessly.
Be there!
Be there!
Be there!

. . . Morning So Soon, Too Soon . . .

I woke up this morning
        /my woman in my mouth/
Making lunch of left-over need
Oozing through a thigh—
My mind a barbed-wire camp of fear,
My privacy exposed to the silent gossip
Of nosey noiseless walls—
A dent beside me in the bed,
Ploughed sheets . . . one earring,
My chilled-filled arm amputated
Up to where your neck withdrew
From the refrigerator of night—
My eyes slits of soft fire
Sword-fighting the sun,
The moon mockingly hovering
In one window of a flashback:

Morning, Lord, so soon, too soon . . .

Love as Nostalgia:
Love as Remembrance

Listening to Horace Silver's "Lonely Woman"

Trained/drained hands at a keyboard
Sprinkling shades of salt
Into niches of an old love
Into silk-masked wounds
Historical throbbing—
Pain of piano nights
Sour mornings . . .
And a bass walks through horror chambers
Of the heart's museum
As scales & notes numb a visiting need,
Rekindle nostalgia and resurrect ghosts
Ground into memory's junkyard—
Plunk out paradoxical acoustics . . .
An old love
An old love
Staggering through smoke
Smogged ideas
Pollutants of worry . . .
Tiptoeing across quicksands,
Tried hands narrow
To crevices of ire and desire,
Nestle with night
Into burning blackflame
Whose final finger (and flicker)
Plucks keys of conch/us mourning:
Black & white notes of nostalgia
Crowding a clandestine vacuum
In one wall of the heart
One ventricle of memory
One well of tears
An old love
An old love

Highflown: Love

In the highflown language
Of moon travelers
Social scientists sort our hurts—
Add their smog-crippled vision—
And rearrange our private pains
Along the Wall Street of current demands;
And my people become the
Cocaine that makes America high:
Become dreams
America sucks through maniacal straws of sleep;
Discounting our lore,
The scientists say we *cannot love*
        Say our needs are numbed:
But sometimes,
When you construct knots in my throat
And your lips re-create my heartclock,
I am hypnotized by the aggregate passion
Of my past   by the sum of my historical ecstasy:
A power we know
Cannot be stilled by airborne theories of scholars
Nestled in Freudian citadels:
A power that cannot be seen
Heard
Or flattened to fit the pages of a book.

SECTION SEVEN
Funky-Grace
(From *The Eye in the Ceiling*)
Mid to Late 1970s

EBR and Katherine Dunham in East St. Louis. 1985.

Myth Vaulter

From the Introduction to
Keith Jefferson's *Hyena Reader*
March 22, 1976

Another Myth-vault, Keith/Jefferson—
Blackpiper, Wordquilter, Warmthbringer,
Wailteller, Deepreaper—
flaunts his
"Mr. 5 by 5"
"Clyde McPhatter"
"Bird"
with flinchless Soulo-Elegance:
 Jazz takes it.
 Jazz takes it away.
 Jazz takes it apart. distinguishes
 the essentials
 from what would be mist.
Rhymes anciently, this finesser,
For a questing/questing hyena
("who's laughing at who?");
talks of air that "wraps its shiny arms around me"
& how the "Pregnant aroma of living"
drives a dart-of-a-blackbody
whose "spine is a spear."

Jefferson knows the boards
and splinters of life:
"you like it deep don't you night";
"veined ghetto"; "Untidy Cheetahs";
"through the nappyhead of night"—
into eternal unw/rappings of love,
dispossession, lust and *Festivities*.

Jefferson, he lifts fog
from the brain and dust
from thirsty party floors:
Better yet, hear Keith Jefferson *Reed!*
Yaw Kay? . . . All Rite!

Bye-Centennial:
Unreflected Thrusts and Frontiers

for Ahaji Umbudi

Drum & Fife
Drum & Fife
Zig America zag
Thru goulash and gumbo and oboe
Patchpatchwork HUM clock
Clockclocking: Tambourine underbump
HUM
HUM
Indelicacies into frontiers
New England
New Africa
New World wading in weeping in antique fears
HAIL!
HAIL!
The seismic lull of liberated bells

Post-toasties
Grape-nuts
Loan Rangers   Jumpingfrogs   Bluespeople
  Allegheny go-go Stradivarian hoe-down Expresso-bo-bo
Mumbling muskets   Ahab in search of Jonah   How kkkum?
  Black gold   Rock-a-my-soul in the bosom of slavery
Ramble of the Pre-amble   DRUM & FIFE   HUM HUM
Into frontiers
  Ace or Spade?   Harborer harborer pearls & harbors
Igloo   Angola & Reggae   Harvest moons/sniper moons
Bus of Bust!

What did Hoo/doo
To get so black & blue
Zig zag
Zig zag

Celluloid transplants
Sutures on the liberty knell
Knockknockknock of night-leerers
                    come to order silence

HUM
HUM
Indelicacies into frontiers
Slapped leather & totemized saddles
Zigzagging hair-triggered lover
Heavyhymn of a naturalborn death-wish
Samboo-boo dance at JamesTown
Soot-stained Oedipal clutch of Jolson

The squeak/squeak of Watergate
Attucks-the-bullet-eater
Attucks-the-bullet-eater
Attucks-the-bullet-eater
Attucks-the-bullet-eater
Attucks-the-bullet-eater
Attucks-the-bullet-eater

HUM
HUM
Emphysema of the drum
Influenza of the fife

HUM HUM
HUM HUM

Flight From Texarkana to Dallas:
Air Edifice

Homage to an Ebony Flight Attendant
August 20, 1977

In the aisle of a giant bee
       stinging and winging clouds
A dextrous, glory-angled, brownflame
Calmed and collected our
       unmumbled apprehension
Into the cushioned hamlet of her face

While the humid murmur-weep of
Texas gaped from the green yawn below:
       grace-girl: helm-lady,
       flesh-edifice . . .
Murmur-weep that clung
To sweating mirages aboard
This plantation in the air
       grace-girl
Where feebled or fancied hands
Clasped mint-juleps
Dispensed from the
Fingers of an ageless ark of flesh:
       grace-girl: helm-lady,
       ebony-edifice . . .
Double-fated flight: on which
Some sat snugly
Assured ancient order *prevailed*—
Even if tested by airborne
       freedom-marchers.

Less snug, and cautiously masking
Their bubbling elations, however,
The deeper-pitched passengers

Hailed *honey-hued grace-girl* with
Silent praises and appellations:
Coolly rejoicing at this revolution—
Fleshingmagically before their eyes!

witnesses . . . witnesses

Meanwhile,
Jubilee-daughter—
Her soft armor impenetrable
As she led the silentchoral ascent—
Knew and unknew the
Cathartic turbulences
Illuminated by her aura:
Maintained her glory-limp—

her lush electricity
her charismatic cause

Remained & Remained:
Effortless in the Brilliant *Dream-amble:*
Inalienable, I tell you,
And Inevitable.

Double Clutch Lover

". . . let me blues ya fo' I lose ya."
Southend saying, East St. Louis, Illinois

Her fury and her fire was in her cold-cold fame:
Double mojo-mama, Yeah, and Double Clutch Lover was her
  name.

She had the cold-cuttin fire, baby, she had the flame, the
  flame.

Her rep was hep—and she didn't mess with no lame—
                Her fire was in her fame!
                Her fire was in her fame!
O Yeah! Uh Huh! O Yeah! Uh Huh!
        Cause she was a double
I said a double / / two barrels
I said a double / / two barrels
        Make it two, babeeeee!
    Cause she was a Double Clutch Lover
And she could double clutch / / clutch-clutch
                double clutch / / clutch-clutch / / your love
                Double-clutcher
                Double-clutcher

She was a, *ah, er-ruh,* triple dealer,
                And a—uuh-uhh—banana peeler,
                        Yeah, a quick-shifting wheeler.
                Double-Clutch Pearl
                Kitchen-Grease Girl
Witch-woman-of-a-healer!

Fruit, funk and fire was in her cold, Lawd!, cold cuttin flame;
She kept comin, kept comin in Jesus' name!
    Double-Clutch Double-Clutch my love

She took my temperature with a two-foot tongue
That accelerated my engine when it reached my lung!
Clutch-Clutch Double-Clutch
A break-fast filly that couldn't be tamed . . .
Couldn't be tamed!
African back-bender that made the Holy Ghost shame:
For Shame! Double-Clutch
For Shame! Double-Clutch
Rump-queen that conquered the washing machine
(Yeah, before it was invented!)
Washboard wonder-woman scrubbing her convictions,
Hand-clapping her way through old-time restrictions:
Knuckle-Rubber
Knuckle-Rubber
Double-Clutch-Lover
Double-Clutch-Lover . . .

Woman walked across fire and still didn't fidget!
Walked across fire, *John Yo Henry,* and still didn't
fidget!
Dig it! Dig it!

Funk-junction lady with a jack-knife jump!
I said a funk-junction lady with a jack-knife jump!
If you can't sprout your tree before she counts to three
She might leave you with a stump:
Funk-junction lady with a jack-knife jump,
Hump-hump / / Hump-hump

Yeah!, yall, her fire, her fire, was in her cold-cold fame
Where Hard-Hearted Hanna couldn't stake no claim:
Double-Clutch-Lover
Double-Clutch-Lover
Lawd, make you run for cover . . .
Hover-hover, baby, hover-hover.
She can gun you to the curb;
Make you *scream-cry* for reverb!

Now ain't that some nerve!
            Girl got nerve!
Double-clutch woman armed with life—
Double-Clutcher, yeah, armed to the teeth with life, Lawd!
            Expert on Strife!
            Expert on Strife!

A triple dealer!
Banana peeler!
Quick-shifting wheeler!
            Double-Clutch-Lover
        Run for cover, man,
        Run for cover, man:
Keeps her foot on my pedal—
            Pushin-clutchin // pushin-clutchin
Keeps her hand on the throttle of life,
            Expert on Strife, Throttle of Life, Expert on Strife.

Funky-Grace
From *The Hero Series*

for Joseph E. Harrison

He took the lion-lunge,
Hey! Hey!
He took the tiger-step,
Hey! Hey!
He took the tomb-trail,
Hey! Hey!
He took the sacred-plunge.
Hey! Hey!

He made the ocean-leap!
Hey! Hey!
He made the gong/gong-call!
Hey! Hey!
He made the death-mouth,
Hey! Hey!
He made the freedom-creep.
Hey! Hey!

He ate the juicy-blues!
Hey! Hey!
He ate the rat/roach flat!
Hey! Hey!
He ate the numb-stare,
Hey! Hey!
He ate the airborne-shoes!
Hey! Hey!

He caught the sassy-space!
Hey! Hey!
He caught the totem-call!
Hey! Hey!

He caught the kill-flame!
Hey! Hey!
He caught the Funky-Grace!
Hey! Hey!
He caught that Funky-Grace!
Hey! Hey!
He caught that Funky-Grace!
Hey! Hey!

New York Seizures

for Raymond Patterson

#1

I sit in a glass submarine
Watching contortion consume beauty
      As flesh inches toward dust and oblivion,
      . . . a-what-a-ya-wanna, eh!? a-what-a-ya-wanna!
      As flesh inches toward the next corner of tumult—
To where wrinkled octogenarians,
      Spontaneous in their gloom,
Stagger-stab the grimacing city blocks
With lock-legged steps
And broken winds exhale columns of creaking
Epilogues from eyes without age . . .

      No dozer, no-doze city and never-wink wailer,
      Babbling through your Benzedrine and beer!

#2

Now disguised as a street lamp,
I am whiplashed/whiplashed into serpentine ecstasy
By lush scenarios
By concrete choruses
      And asphalt furies:
By the snaking quarrel of bi-lingual taxi-cabs—

      Where the night turns yellow!
      Where New York gets mel-looow!

—And perspiring tenements:

Toombs for pre-people returning home
From mystical voyages to be somebody

By the hover-clusters of chuckling midgets
Who hurl diabolical ringshouts under thunder-tears
Of Gleeful gods: Apollo, Shango, John Henry & Bobo—
And rocket naughty clichés at bronze brickhouses,
Headhunters
Plush stallions,
Stark-deniers of identities,
Penis-flingers
Cunt-lubricators,
Sweetboys
& Blood-borrowers:

> *ennie meenie mynie mo las night/night befo*
> *spin yo bottom shoot yo shot keep her'n creep her*
> *let me blues ya fo I lose ya let me try ya*
> *'fo I buy ya I got the jones 'nnn if you got*
> *the bones dick haarrddd as Chinese Arithmetic*
> *ya know I ain't tawkin bout yo momma wit hu good*
> *o soul . . . uh uhhh! uh uhhhh! uh uhhhhhh!*

#3

The neighborhood nextdoor is hallucinating:
Woman says she saw a BlackJesus riding in a WhiteHog
Wearing a Green jumpsuit and holding two BrownFoxes;
A platinum barrel of death stares into the stomach
Of a short-order cook demanding the cashregister & life, *to go!*
A gentleman who wears low profiles tells his woman
That she makes love like his best buddy;

A Puerto Rican speaks Voodoo with an African accent;
A European speaks African with a Spanish accent;
A West Indian yawns in Yiddish and curses in Arabic;
An African speaks English in silence;
A slave revolt occurs under the cover of a blackout;
Color-crossed lovers hold hands in cross-eyed Central Park;
Subway trains are flying nonstop to South Africa;
Harlem has received the Nobel Prize for Peace;
Mountain climbers are trying to scale the City Debt;
The Indians are hijacking the Empire State Building;
This winter's snow turns out to be co-caine.

                                                    #4

Lucid lumbrous eye
          New York;
Luminous fragments,
          Like New Year's Eve tin-foils,
          Collect into an epidemic of flesh-ignited candles
That refuse to go out—
Even when the temperamental gods of Con-Edison are
     comatose;

Whir-City, heat forest
Of memorable fevers,
          Asphalt icon:

Jezzibel mesmerizer,
Sleep-exempt entrancer:
I rap-prance my congratulations on the achievement of your
     excellent madness,
On the triumph of your pretty contradictions;

I tap-dance my salutes through your basement of
shuttles and
       barbiturates;
I clop-clop along your rib-cage of cobblestones;
I pee-pee in the wee-wee hours of your doorways;
I mee-lee in your disco-drudgery;
I be-me in your awesome amber:

      No dozer, no-doze city & never-wink wailer,
      Babbling through your Benzedrine and beer!

SECTION EIGHT
Long Distance Warriors, Dreamers & Rhymers
1980s to 2010

Gwendolyn Brooks's 70th Birthday. (L-R) Darlene Roy, EBR, Gwendolyn Brooks, Haki R. Madhubuti, Shirley LeFlore, Sherman L. Fowler. Chicago, Illinois. 1987.

Long Distance Warriors, Dreamers & Rhymers

In memory of my parents,
John Henry & Emma Jean Redmond
(& for Mahmoud El Kati)

O classical mammas & poppas: soular-centered lovers &
Parents of Drum Scripture & Pyramid:
                Nile-cool & Benin-blue Songhaifiers:
                hip—& pre-Hip/Hop—diasporan daddies
                    & *honey-in-the-rock divas:*
              ship-huddled & cattle hurried
        across the Ethiopian Ocean. O epic parents:

Fine brown arks war-poised & prayerful. Long-distance
        Dreamers
& W.E.B.'s *souljahs* smelting ancestral ore
              into double-conscious Rhymes
                 of epic Passage
                        epic Pain
                            epic Spillage:

Lo, you *stolen legacies* Rocking burdens beside the Mississippi
        & creeping or racing
                like Ogun's archers & Harriet's scouts
                    through *steal-away* nights:

Militantly upright, or shape-shifty, your *winged whisperings*
arming us with clouds of *joy* that "swing low" & "fetch high":

    Olmec & SoulTrek   Nat Turner & Sojourner
              Paul Laurence Dunbar & James Weldon Johnson
    Hughes' Blues   Mahalia & Maya   B.B. & Cee Cee
              Mary Bethune & Henry Dumas & Duke's Jive
    Zora Neale & Larry Neal   Cullen & Hayden
              Elijah & Umoja   Gwendolyn & Aretha

Kenyatta & Mandela   Nyere & Amiri   Nina & Sonia
Toni & Terri   Malcolm & Jesse
Katherine & Latifah   Juju & Jesus

O parents of Mem/Wars & Love-Mergers: ritual (!) clickings
storefront-saviors   cornbread-fantasies   hambone & banjo
railroad & gumbo   Thurgood's legions   King's cadres
of Orators...O epic parents of mother-shore & father—ore
smelting generations of fine brown arks
into battle & prayer: warriors dreamers rhymers.

Nine by Nine

Nine Haiku for Katherine Dunham on her 92nd Birthday

Lords of London legs
Fly the Queen's chariot through
Nine decades and change

Drum-spangled feet greet
A century of applause,
Accolades, musings

Thirty-three thousand
Five hundred eighty days of
Romance, grief & art

Her Manor (manner): "Woman
With a Cigar" pours "Cakewalk(s)"
On "Floyd's Guitar Blues"

Divine meets profane
At rites de "Missa Luba"
"Barrelhouse" & Jazz

Haute dramaturgy
Abides multiclassical
Curves & ethnic oeuvres

Love-laced comminglings:
"Carib Song(s)," East Saint Louis,
Chicago, Dakar

Vévé of Shango
Apropos Tokyo, Port
Au Prince, Paris

Choreo-gumbo
At her 92nd floor-
Show, hey, Ayíbobo!

Choreo/Cosmos-Empress'
Leg-a-cy Lands on East Saint Earth

Apropos Katherine Dunham

I

Of Katherine. Her century. This homage.
To her leg-a-cies her divine sashays her Legba/s.
To her life struts her Shay Shays her life-marks.
To her drum-mobiles her loa-residences.
To her conch/us/nest her woman's work
her wakefulnest.

II

Of this Lady undulator imprinting
the metroplex with cosmophonic leg-lore:
shuttling between East Boogie
& invisible provinces of Vodun.

Of a "possessed" oba-diva romancing multi-tonal
shadows reborn as figurines as flesh.

Of Sisterserpentine & the slowdragging Yanvalou
snaking through "stormy weather"
& bluesplendent "cabins in the sky."

Of Madame Gong Gong's stomp ring shout tongue
bump tap cakewalk ball chain jerk.

Of Lady curator excavating lost countries.
Of Madame rivergrinder
& corn-bread midwife to the blues.
Of the the Mysteries' Choreographer:
choreographer to the Oracles.

Of East River Orb: Witch-queen of TenthStreet:

Temple-founder: Swordswoman: Drumpriestess:
Caribbeanologist: Damballah's lover:
Born again Civil-warrior.

Of Chariots of legs engulfed in wings:
Leg-a-sees: her cosmic transport & metronome.

III
Of Katherine's choreopera
descending to East saint Earth
in a Port Au Princely slink:

"Hambone" to "Minnehaha"
"Sally Walker" to "L 'Ag Ya!"

Of Katherine's leggage? Katherine incarnate:
peripatetic museums, stilt-walking archives,
drum-stung zombies, rum-drenched desires
circumnavigating torsos,
serpentine twist of sweat-sweet libations.

IV
Of 532 North 10th Street (her Sixties-centered
ambience):
a plie away from Mor Thiam's djembe
& her namesake Museum & Workshop
where children glitter in choreogardens
near brash heaps of human litter.

Of a fresh century inheriting the largesse
of her leg-a-cies,
reconnecting estranged continents,
leg-a-sees for the legions
goom-bopping their shout-outs
to the Ballerina of East Boogie.

V
Of her century & this homage.
Her century & Langston's. Margaret Walker's.
Zora's & Melvin B. Tolson's. T.S. Eliot's. And Duke's.
Her century & Ruth St. Denis's. Isadora Duncan's.
Du Bois's. And Martha Graham's.

Of her century. Its riot of memories.
Child eyes drunk on nightskies & a special star.
The awakening hiss shout sting of colorlines.
Of God's Glen Ellyn & AME's Joliet.
Chicago's gumbo of causes: Its cult kingdoms
& upSouth promised lands: drumJive
& carryovers.

Its Cube and dance theaters. Its Negro Ballet.
Its WPA. Its Richard Wright. Canada Lee. Studs
Turkel.
Its Ludmilla Speranzeva. Baptist Bulwarks
& Rosenwald Foundation: Its havens
from Hitler's Reich.

Of Katherine's life-length paradigm:
a splicing of anthropology & dance.

VI
Of our worlds as her stages:
Ageless Africa in the Round. Of 1930's New York
& Negro Evenings. Europe as Little Theater.
Of London's Darling. Paris's Esprit Noir.
Amsterdam's Empress. Senegal's Isis.
Haiti's Priestess of Meringue. Tokyo's Ebony Geisha.
East Saint Africa's Choreographer Laureate.

VII
Katherine's century as Sister-precursor:
MTV BET Video Breakdance:
Mega/funk- & dunk-a-delia of Alvin James Tina Patti
Michael Debbie. And Yo-Yo.

VIII
Her century. And Sterling Brown's.
Their *Negro Caravan*. Bojangles's. Josephine's.
Buckminster Fuller's. Miles Davis's.
Ours.

IX
Out of her century this homage:
Bluescript. Hymnal of Arias & Gutbuckets.
Ode of East Boogie. A squatter's tale. Of Choteau.
Tenth Street. State Street in Hawkville.

Of diamond-twinkle Katherine. Her leggage.
Of visions blending like rainbows
& curling up into flames:
& in the contagious wink of a thigh or feather
rising like gospel to engulf
our brilliant grievings and strivings:
To choreograph the loa's bidding.

Reginald & Edna Petty Host a Soiree for Artists at Their East Saint Love Castle

A Poetic Recapitulation

Piano's genius Eugene Haynes Jr., enters the Pettys'
Castle of Tall-Talking Spirits & beholds a Diasporan
Expo fit for His Excellency: candles, totems, fabrics,
Tiled walls, trees, masks, & bi-state warrior-artists—cool as
Kenyans—moving like Seventies' 'Groove' Things
                    Yeah-yeah!

Sunshine's systolic Ensemble trilling His ears with
Djembes, bi-lingual congas, barreldrums & shakeres.
Ethno-gumbo buffets rippling with ideological
Doo-wop & surrealucisous cuisines . . .
Tanzanian Ugali taunting Ghanaian tongues.
Jolof & Pilaf rice/s simmering in drumbellies.
Conch/us gastronomes savoring post-apartheid
Reparations, collard green salad & brown rice.
Cayenne-sweetened Gospel Bird flying soulo from
Popeyes, Lee's & Ponderosa. Chapungu
Sculpture Park shape-shifting into BBQ-flavored
Laughter, hot tamales, ground nut stew, sorghum/
Cheese bread, olive oil dressing & cantaloupe.
Writers, fabric makers, musicians, poets, arts
Leaders, translators & ceramicists prancing
Around wine punch like bodies
                    In a Soular Gallery.

Zimbabwean blue tones wooing French-Wolof (ian)
Nasalities. Silk screened intellectuals cross-
Pollinating with agbadas, peppered beans, kufis,
Balding revolutionaries, sandals, wigs/braids/perms
—Tikis w/dashikis draping Sixties refugees—&
Faithful East Saint Love
            Embracing its expatriates:

Tall Day/Tall-Talk on Lincoln Avenue, north of Jones
Park—recalling those "we shall overcome" summers
Of heat & hatred—in the Pettys' Garden of Equanimity:
Cherry pie strolling ancestrails with rice balls, fruit
Salad, strawberries, vanilla ice cookies w/sprinkles:
Soulfestive Royalty,
Feasting with fingers, munching on—& inventing—
Memories, imbibing fables that fall like twinkles
From Haynes' Sahara-wide eyes . . . mirages of
John Robinson, Lucy & Fannie Turner, 1917's
Holocaust, Taylor Jones III, Miles Davis & Leon
Thomas . . . moving like Seventies' "Groove Things, Yeah.
                    Yeah-yeah!"

Indigenous Daughter Awake
in the Dreams of Nana

indigenous daughter's heart spoke through her eyes
upon her dream-brilliant arrival
     curled like a *pearl*
in the womb of wartime East St. Louis

her Gregoryan chants,
syncopated stitches of a homespun pastiche,
emerged from gardens, green thumbs, cigar trees, clean
  dirt yards,
train whistles, bard Dunbar's Elementary School,
hymns & street corner oracles

from her 14th street fo'c'sle,
she scoped the hives of jive & ethics of sweat
floating between 13th Street & Boismenue & Colas Avenues

navigated dutiful daughter-hours
through oceans of dictionaries, bibles & dishwasher

girlwhirled in the family gyre
of activists, composers, educators, polyglots & farmers
—several Milky Ways from Ladue—
she became Bond Avenue's Trumpeted Valedictorian,
sandwiched between Miles & Jackie at Lincoln High,
then hurdled the Mississippi & climbed
the Phi Beta Kappa staircase at Washington University

began exploring God's sleeping provinces,
looking for hidden countries of opportunity

became daughter-mother & astute parent
scholar-mother & astute parent
lawyer-mother & astute parent

le grand mother & astute nana
with seed & thread she sewed credos
of tolerance into mosaics of commitment,
volunteering her heart to bi-state & bi-cultural causes,
forbid the River be a divide—
but an arterial song of reciprocal transfusions

spiritual homebody circling her son/s—& their gardens—
& stitching petite stems of love
into the habitations of newly encountered spheres

quilted families by hand & washed them in joy-boiled tears
before pegging them to the stars
& ecstatically flying to remotely accessible
heights of music, drama, opera, jazz—
remaining un-at-home in airplanes

versatile defender of underlived lives,
nana,
empowered flowered from the garden of King Alfred &
  Queen Mary
nana,
whose heart, cuddling a bouquet of green thumbs,
speaks through her eyes
speaks through her eyes

For Peggy Ann (Gregory) Newman on her 55th Birthday, June 30, 2000
Commissioned by Sheila Stix

Robert Allen/Kathleen Cleaver/
Abdul Alkalimat

SAYEN . . .
 "Art to the power black!"—

Old guard Negro-euro arts & power blackened—en guard!—
like gunpowder into pantherized, lumpen murals of Malcolm
RAM BAM FESTAC & InnerCity ASCACs—jammin'
fuselages of pride spillage politics and poetry,
three-eyed warrior-dreamers sleepwoke in dyen cryen
   tryen time,
no-shit no-quit no-split time . . .

Following a conference revisiting the Black Power Movement, University of Illinois,
Urbana-Champaign, 2006.

Every Blood's Avery Brooks

Hawk, finding Ankh Dumas
redemptive, black-nestled
& plentiful, be

came everyman's
cruise control & site-setter,
compass aboard brooding arks . . .

In Memoriam: Fresh Ancestors

the gods' home-grown stalwarts
are looping our memory—
        Coretta, Ossie, Yolanda—
leaving us grace & taking leave of wars

now, o ancient, umoja-exemplars,
grace these fresh ancestor-couriers
with earth- & sky-filled High byes

with grace-arched imani-drums
for stone & iron paths
deliver their soft-steel selves to drum-heavens

Tommy's Haiku . . . Tommy's Elegy

eclectic as Duke
whose A Trane/caravan you
ride bop-stride, homeboy

Ars Americana, 1996
Haiku cum Tanka

Toni Cade Bambara
(1939-1995)

Fresh ancestress struttin death:
You & You-After—
Guerilla, My Love

Ameri-Amour #1

Oklahoma shrine's
Love-blown mind drifts: Waco to
"Ghetto" to Waco
As the zombie of Jonestown
Dances solo with Sundown

Entitled

Jerome Rothenberg's
TECHNICIANS OF THE SACRED
Discovered FOUND poems
Shook songs from bow pumpkin bow(e)ls
ARS ETHNOPOETICA

Ina Peabody, Sister Friend

In Memoriam

wherever Ina went there was music . . .

whether she hopscotched from pigtails to fairytales

>   or flexed her girlish grin
>   tinged with a righteously wicked consciousness

whether she stalked her dreams like a Duke Ellington tune

>   or savored Life like a gourmet,

Ina, the modest jazzologist,

>   carried Bird, Billie & Miles on her tongue
>   & volumes of books in her head

moving between the open stacks of love
& the open roads of memory . . .

Southend sage, balancing libraries & blues,
>   Rush City & Athens
>   East Boogie & Bougainvillea
>   Piggott Street & the Milky Way
>   Goosehill & Green Dolphin Street
>   Tenth Street Tech & MIT
>   Lincoln Park & Cutty Sark

wherever she went the music led & followed

>   Ina, sister-sophisticate,
>   tasted Life "Straight—No Chaser,"

feasted on elegance, mental riots,
revolution, thin books with thick characters,
collard greens & limousines, . . .

heavy lady, serious sister—even in light weather,

wherever Ina is . . .   there is music . . .

Maya Toni Alice
3 blue haiku

          snubbing doom/seven women
    fret! rise! ! glow—ntu
maya angelou

howard cornel princeton u's
    sula's warts, pilot's blues
[sweet] lorain's jazz-tart hues

        god's zeal like zora's
           yields gluttonous famines:
                oxymorons purple bronze

A Writer's Retreat at Maya Angelou's Overlaps National Black Theatre Festival

A Poetic Recollection

Hearing Ossie Davis warble like *atumpan*/talking drum
Wasn't a treat I foresaw when I tucked East St. Louis
Into the helm of my thoughts & sailed toward Winston-
        Salem to woodshed with poetry.
Following a wedding/stop in New Jersey I settled on
        Maya's Valley Road Island
& nibbled on a monastic regimen of
        5 am calisthenics & jazz.
Then, each day, while the sun floated like a slave ship
To the horizon, dirt trails in nearby Bethabara park
        Quenched my feet's
                Thirst for the pulse of trees;
& back at Maya's Island, I bathed, debriefed, toasted
Henry Dumas' muses
                & slumbered all day in poetry.
Excepting repasts with Dolly McPherson or Angelou,
& love bouts with Asian cuisinarts,
                I word-feasted & people-fasted . . .
Until waves of Tom Feelings' Middle Passage
Hemorrhaged brilliantly on my solitary canvas.
        [He'd bussed to the Festival from Columbia, SC,
        To Cheer friend Carl Gordon's Achievements
        & listen to the pithy oratures of Jan Carew.]

        Then, opening glitterama!
& gauntlets of Aldridge, Robeson, Hansberry & Ailey
Descended like *deus ex machina* upon Winfield, Ossie,
Woodie & Faison; with Cicely-in-residence leading a
Long Distance Dream of "colored girls": Micki Grant
Dawn Lewis, Sheryl Lee Ralph, Sandra Reeves-Phillips,
Vanessa Bell Calloway, "lion walking" Ntozake . . .
Followed by dues-steep acoustics of Earl Hyman,

Dick Anthony Williams, Charles Dutton, William
Greaves, Malcolm Jamal Warner & Bill Duke—jazz-
   Layering R&B epics with HipHop ghettoglyphics.

                  Seasoned with poetry's scarifications,
Winston-Salem sun, battle-chiseled dialog of black
   Thespians, Sister Maya's high grain hospitality,
Ossie's drum-in-cheek wit, Joseph Marcell's blues-
   Tinted face & the blasé genius of Ed Bullins,
I climbed into the cockpit of my soulo craft
                  & Soared back to East Boogie.

Looking Through the MayaScope II

Madame Angelou
My how your arkestras grow
Cultivating
Syncopations in drum-rich seeds
Of afterglow

Sister-phenom & the planet's most popular poet
Maya intones her spicy continuum
Of crooners divas bluesicians & diviners
—Heroic/sheroic/euphoric—
Cookin' on the anvil of her tongue
Shape-shifting into bop-phat singers & swingers
Gettin' merry like Kwanzaa

From "festivals & funerals" come the syncopated sashays
Of her verbs & nouns, soulo choruses
Strummed up & drummed up from rivers
Of religion, war, & romance

By her own testimony, a literary archeologist,
Maya shepherds the planet's tribes,
Imbibes their nectar of song & gong,
Takes the pulses of their mournings,
Then serenades the Soular System—
From the funkadelic to the psychedelic

Bardic & Bluesplendent in her Badness
She trills & swills elemental tales
Into contrails of elegant guitar language—
Cinematographic, lyric-lushious
& wakeful in their rises, layers, & logics!

Culinary sorceress whose poetic pastiche
Includes a pinch of sun, a spoon of moon,
A half cup of laughter, a dash of dozens,

A gulp of bible, a bite of blues,
A rib of cage, a length of chain, a smooch of eyes,
A slice of nightmare, a pint of prayer

Rising from her kitchen, she casts the poet's brush
Upon the variegated canvas of our passions,
Prances, fences, & scats as voluminous memoirist,
Jazzologist, cultural philanthropist,
Pro bono lover, polyglot, freedom-sprite
& third-eyed ancestor-convener
Who wouldn't take nothing for our journeys
—or our jams

Swordswoman, Maya marinades & curates
The succulent terrain of our dreams,
Covers our backs in thick battle or thin rain

Sister of the eulogistic joy!
O Phenomenal Word Fiddler O!

My Maya Angelou
How your arkestras grow
Cultivating
Palpitations as anticipations glow

Now comes Hush before Song that Springs Spirit
& Heart-Shout-Out: Joy! Maya!

Maya's Kitchen: Homage to SisterCook

Maya's cookin' again . . . & we,
      epicurious old salts & newly seasoned/newly wrought,
voyage thru her kitchens as words,
      roasting like turkey on her tongue,
roll over lips of her oven & feed our famished minds
with loaves of poetry,
(purple) onion rings of biography,
        tart salads of song & yeasty yields of drama.
As we sample baklava & a sheaf of kwansabas,
      hair rises & struts on the backs of our heads
like Arkansas corn stalking Arkansas skies. And in our
  eco-culinary ecstasies,
we curve like freight trains 'round some bend,
bending & blending a howler's moan
into an unending tome of grace, funk & glory,
into ever farthest jazzgasms
      spitting out years like a backfiring T-Model
      traded for a Rolls Royce,
like Tobacco Road traded for Valley Road.

Maya's cookin' again . . . marinating nightmares in memwars...
      in Stamps & Stockton, Sonoma & Sacramento, Harlem
& Oakland,
      in Cairo & Accra, Winston-Salem & Miami, Kingston &
KC, fufu in St. Loo,
      in Bellagio & Berkeley, Athens & Atlanta, Paris & Pacific
Palisades, Cancan in San Fran,
      in Wichita & Seattle, London & Los Angeles,
      Le Cordon Bleu in haiku.

Maya's cookin' again . . . in *Cabarets to Freedom* . . . culling
  hymns for hearths.
Poems from fryin' pans. Stories from stove tops. Hopping John
  griots from gritty grills.
Patty cake graces from childhood aces.

Short stacks of tall tales from flat irons that wail.
Saucy sermons from pre-heated prayers. RSVP's from respect-
   glazed airs.
Corn pone triptych from a coal-burning rack.
        Smothered blues from a delta skillet—black.
Loosin' lyrics from a rope of bratwurst. Songified similes for a
   cool water thirst.
Shish kebobs of ballads from a skewer's rod. Second line dirges
   from a first line of god.
        Spicy proverbs from a rush of pepper soup.
        Folk talk from a high stalk of fresh green dew.
        Lusty verse of brew from peanut stew.
Rotisserie of revelry from a spit turning slow.
        A Creole/gumbo soulo flo' show from a bayou mojo.
A gourmet-of-an-essay from a micro-ray.
Fine line of china from a kitchen in North Carolina.

Maya's cookin' tonight:
Proof's in metaphors we've plucked from tunnels & heights
   to bake anthems & epics for familistic rites.
Under strobes & frennels made of stars & scars, we strutted
   kitchen stages
with the mean & cream of soul cuisine.
Churning nouns into verbs, she said we'd
   sister & brother each other.

Blue-Eyed Sula Sings Solomon's
Song Among Beloved Tar Babies

for Toni Morrison
(who knows how to shimmy
who knows how to shake)

LADY GRIOT
     of the
Infrastructural
     yarn

Who dares to

turn a stone
dust a broom

raise a rug
raise a roof

shake a leg
break a leg

lame a myth
tilt a lie

     Rite Reverend Priestess of Know/Mads
     Sonorous hipsichordist of the Humble Regal Hymns:
          for Bessie   for Isis and Frances
          for Josephine   for Zora and Langston
          for Pecola   for Phyllis and Fats

Folk-la-la O this manna of Fictionist!
Bop-Bent Insurrectionist! FunkLuscious got-to-go-to-meeting:

Shimmy in the wee-grind
Scat in the key-hole
Murmur in the pee-hole

Emerald Mouth/Blues-Eyed Woman
Of Blood & Awe,
Toni Sights/sees through/us
Ntu Our Future-swum river-sermons and hindshores

Our daughters keeper
Our sisters keeper
Our mothers keeper

Oshun
Sapphire
Big Mama
Nefertiti
Sula
Urzuli

Sweet-somber elliptical sorceress
Piloting *Song of Solomon*

Gone and pilot for us Girl!
O midwife of divas and dangers

Umbilically
Bonded by words
Blinded by words
Strangled by words
Released by words

Pleasures w/rapped in god-concentric jujus

in Gumbo
Cobalt
Funkincense

Broken masks and shards of colonial clones . . .
        Toneless and Un-atoned
            Leavings

      Armed with your litany of *Tar Babies*

Reloadable Fusilages of Digestible
        And Unregrettable anguishes

      Ogres Broiling in Spiritual Ovens

Cool Infernos
           Resurrected
                    As Other Honorable Secrets—

      & Private Holocaustal Quiets

           Such as the Embalming of the Bland

laming of myths
tilting of lies

We hear you Toni

(EBR's introduction of Toni Morrison for the River Styx PM Series, April, 1985, Washington University's Edison Theater, St. Louis, MO.)

His Eminence Plays
The Soular System

(Following recording session: Hammett Bluiett
with cameo appearances by LadySmith Black
Mambazo, Hugh Masekela and Quincy Troupe—
NYC 7/7/87)

kora kora hear the strings attached
whining wires across holy-whittled wood
choral whistles warbling through soulular valves:
CPR for the communiversal flock.

i hear hyena hearts
shrieking in innercantations:

humming umbilical hook-ups
intimations & extensions
soular connectives: sonic blooms

percussive divinations!
diasporan indentations!
bluesplendent scarifications!

hammett i hear you hammett

gutbucketeer:
tonguing the riversax:
inverting the tribal viscera
evoking the metaphysical funk
coaxing the metaphorical flame
bluesplendent: extempore extempore

continuum: connectives:
   archives streams bridges linkages
   retentions survivals ditties
rattle slap roll suck the scrumptious drum
explore implore empower our antiphonal pertinence

soweto kingston harlem
soweto kingston harlem

hear the rooty contrapuntalisman:
masekela mojo masekela
hugh and cry
hugh and sky
here in the wry where riffs writhe i
hear sojourner conching thru
umoja caverns of escape

(lovejoy/brooklyn/madison/east saint love/north
saint luck/the island/fireworks station/kinloch)
kingdoms of escape to holy-roller relief
and from passages low way-weigh low
come the lumbrous/labyrinthine tropes
      of troupe:
      bluescandescent rite-rales reptilic scats

      hammett hugh quincy
      zulu xhosa yoruba
      highlife reggae gospel

      gourds trilling gluttonous memories
      lush descendent-gifts of groove-art:
      hallelujahs hainted by field hollers

ogun
odetta
ogloom
o/moms
obatala
o/bessie
obeah
hound-dog-woman
hooche koochie washboard
john o john yo henry

"can't you hear me . . .
can't you hear me when I call."

Aerolingual Poet of Prey

for Alvin Aubert who surveys
life from the quiet's deep see

Through a two-way telescope of time,
he tracked the stormy calms of history.
carried gravity in his sight. Behind
him stretched a flapping scroll of ir-
reconcilable callings. Before, there
swirled a grinning turret of racial
daggers aiming to splinter the brother-
ing father within him. From gooberdust
rainlore graphite redbeans gut-trails
creole-dreams ink river korean-conflict
mardi-gras typewriter bible nightmare
ritual-rice and computer he forged wings
of discovery wings/of delivery. Gained
griot-height. And orbiting gave birth
to *Obsidian.*

Became poet of prey:
South Lousiana aero-linguist. Resur-
rected life's raw incenses. Re-forged
cool wordbolts. Moved North: Leaned
South. Kept *Feeling Through.* Kept com-
ing smack up *Against the Blues.* Kept
planting earthharp in air.

    In-flight, he drank his brew
    of laments: *trouble-deep rivers*
                river-deep troubles

    In-flight*, skimmed fear off death.*

Poet of prey:
Scavenger who claimed and climbed languages.
Rocked and groaned through love's highlow.
Closed: Opened in the moontime of need. Follow-
ed quick/eccentric dartings. Entered slow/blood-
filled hiding places. Lusted after sizzling carry-
overs. Twitched in the rumble-quiet: In the
sweat-time of riots. Watched the glitter of
upheaval grow sheenless in the logic of
darklight. Wrote. Wished. Salivated. Stayed
Case. Stayed edge. Stayed course.

Poet of prey:
Proper poppa chronicler. Lured concentric
florals of grief into slim sleeves of poetry.
Into rural sheaths of jubilant anger: Into
lyrics of coiled, knowledgeable passion.
into folk-lucid tropes. Holy-evil. Grimace. Twist.

Poet of prey:
Hear his sober ecstasies resonate. See
them levitate midst the heart's acoustics.
Alvin Aubert: clear, spicy, bright babble
made edible as in a gulp of blues. Inhalable
as in the first pungent breeze of gumbo.

Movin' West Tanka

lyric waves flirt with
Califia's shores
& cuddle ear- & eye-paths
as end-land's plural culture-
scapes harbor earth's jazzgasms

Northern California

    (from Texarkana . . .)
Percussive progenitors
    (New Orleans . . .)
def as buffalo soldiers
    (Little Rock . . .)
forge a race-spiced gumbo
    (& Langston . . .)
as they boogaloo west like a gold-rush . . .

Even Tornado Alley's wheat- corn- & coal-stained plains
    gyrate like Dunham's Damballa
as Galveston's Juneteenth jazzes Califia's amazons
    Mama Pleasant's San Francisco
& Sacramento's Women's Civic Improvement Center . . .

From Hunter's Point & Bop City
Oaktown & Oak Park
honor guards & shipyards
City Lights & Del Paso Heights
grapevine & the-Jesus-line
tobacco road & Florin Road . . .
drum-springs juke jump & ejaculate a neo-choreo-mojo
  cosmos
black/kenning books & broadsides (marcus/new
  day/carol's)
scholars/houses/student unions & departments
(berkeley/grove street/hayward/sacto & san jose state)
poetry/panthers/art/caucuses/politics & power . . .

3rd s/whirling/wielding an Afrimexicali Continuum
of Pacific rim shots:
viz: an ethno-sax-o-phono-sermonic-tonic
viz: Sons/Ancestors Players . . .

The Blues Priest of Stowe Way

In memory of James Warren Penn, 1932–1997

sayonara to the blues priest of Sacramento
     (& yo! to a young ancestor)
     who performed his jazz-rites
at Penndell's Place on Stowe Way
     weaving & bobbing like a sermon among
poolside/grill stereo fireplace kitchen & bar

chugalugging chittlins & caviar
     & cheesecake & chasing
them with boilermakers
     rums mum/s tums & perriers

rite reverent truth-stretcher
     & royal crooner of the dozens
—"you know you aint never lied"—
     who never knew a stranger or a loner
—for long

most-host brother of "service": imperially spiffy
     & spit-shined even in battered shorts
& run-over-shoes-for-sandals
     & surrounded by jazz sonorities
menus of a zillion gastronomes
     the *Physician's Desk Reference*
racks of wine & racks of lamb
     & circumcised dreams
of vacationing voyeurs;
     flap-five Jim of butt-strut eloquence:

conductor director safari & flock leader
     of convoys into the labyrinths of **neon**where
& cattle heavens & jazz junkets to Monterey

            Bay-Area-Soularplex Los Angeles w/strings
fever-cool coves along California 101

bohemian partaker of les elegants
            who sedated disbelievers
w/his hip-sofical wink & chic-shaman tones
            whether stowed away on Stowe Way

in RVs cushiony hotel ballrooms
            open air castles condo-hideaways
or sleek Buicks snaking thru midnight's
            midsection to a funky FM thump

boogie bishop who improvised symphunkonies
            doo/bop greasy/street & pulpit operas
translated jail-speak into mumbles clear-jumbles
dominoes & whist: whose J.O.B, was doing time
w/the do-ers of time & jumping bad
            w/the clock-wise raw-wise rough-wise
double-wise & outer-wise

bopriffing Jim & dandy & handy like brandy
            & "daddy" of cats

loaded w/laughter rascality sun's-light
            & moon's-flight

earned life's credits like a college degree

            wore the hashmarks of His Experience
like tattoos

            gulped down knowledge like alcohol's
last call

kept the world under surveillance
with his twinkle-smile

that twinkle-trickster-preacher-smile
hiding a second one cocked like a hammer:

ready to blow you a kiss . . . or blow you away

Don't Bring Him No 'Bad News'

(Poem written on the Occasion of the Retirement of Ike Paggett: Saturday, June 12, 2004, Sacramento, California. Correction: Ike's not your usual Retiree; he's entering a period of "Intellectual Reflection" wherein he can also count his mountains of money!)

main man Ike waves off "bad news" with a musical wan that
   balances his life's roar,
this man-o-war & horn-a-plenty, this man of moment & scope,
   acoustical vistas & hope,
this man of stylized subtleties—reservedly & deservedly hip,
twinkle-eyed maestro & reluctant administrator,
   this man-on-point,
confluence of spices of sound falling into cushioned *dins* of
   symphunkynies,
his baton orchestrating soprano distances between Grambling
   & Grant High,
with a missile base in Turkey rising midway,
as father Ike conjures Valerie, Maisha, & Akilah . . .

rhythm-rife proteges at Sacramento High bloom into jazz
   flowers at Monterey's Festival,
while Ike caucuses with Frank Kofsky, Paul Carter Harrison,
   Mike Gates
& Sons/Ancestors, then whirls in phat flats & arrow-edged
   sharps
swilling in the orature of "The Great McDaddy"—
fertile musical father, Ike, who cultivates fraternal brew at the
   Maja Club,
Mr. D's, A Touch of Class & the artsy fartsy flock of bohemia
   near downtown;
cultivates companeros with names like Jimmy, Lou, Darryl,
Steve, Frank & Johnny (as in Heartsman) . . .

from zones of sound Ike & "Cappy"
   launch "Independent Lady"—
then our bejeweled maestro "conducts" astral orchestras from
   Sacto's Heavenly Studios,
fishing delectable kin-notes from "Bloodlinks & Sacred Places"
& tipping a glass of colored wonder—"straight" as a
   "no-chaser"—
tipping a heady mug of grins,
tipping a horn so surreal & sublime that Maya Angelou asks,
"Eugene, where's that handsome saxophone player . . .
you know, that wonderful looking man?" . . .

Ike's ardent blues overtures blend the jazzaic & the prosaic,
black-based ala 60s & 70s but ecumenical &
   eclectic as Duke Ellington,
as he goes whirling through Third Worlds with Maya,
Art & Hortense Thornton, Jose Montoya
& The Royal Chicano Air Force, Marie Collins
& The Oak Park School of Afro-American Thought . . .
then, two decades later,
   segues into Oak Park Summer Concerts
with Pharaoh Sanders, Leon Thomas, Nancy Wilson,
   Dizzy Gillespie & Coke Escovito . . .
so don't bring him "no bad news"
   cause he'll leverage it with music . . .
main man Ike,
   anchored life-deep in the acoustics of human *heights*,
poised with a baton
   —or musical wan—
   to carry us magically through tragedy
with a triumphant crescendo of grace . . .

A Poetree, A Love Trove, A Village Grove

for The Wedding of Akilah Paggett & Morris Blaylock
Saturday, August 20, 2011, Atlanta, Georgia

> *of aspect & spirit, they are*
> *beautifully-beJeweled in betrothal-tones*
> *like voice-winged Ikettes soaring on*
> *Gloria-arias...*
> > *blues-dreamt, s/woosh-swept &*
> > *s/wishing in a garden of poetrees . . .*

Soul-plated & soul-mated in New World Crowns,
 This bliss-beJeweled & *august* pair,
Groomed in their Old World Ritual Grounds,
 Coo-coo in the rarest of August air . . .

 (*ooo-weee-ooo babee-babee*)

While in their legacy-laced Village Grove,
There glows an honor-laden Love Trove—
Lushed with amply-ancient tree-steep fruits,
Swooned by South-spiced/Sacramento roots . . .

(*Another heart-swelling/eye-welling wedding poem, yes,*
but also a lyrical gong-gong & broom-jumpers' praise-song
from the heroic/sheroic/Ike-onic Village they call home.)

> ala Akilah & Morris . . .
> ala Akilah-Mo' . . .
> ala Mo'-Kilah . . .

> *(Perhaps even a dash of Tequila*
> *to spur their landing on a Moon of Honey . . .)*

A Million Yester-Morrows Ago, Ancestors foresaw Akilah &
Mo'—

      & us, Elders & Kin—
In this *august*/August Tale
      Setting Sail on Ancestrails
& casting Dreamy Wish-Sweetened Wails & Spells
      Into Vibrant-Village-Wells
      Named/claimed by Two Whom Love Befell.

Now as we fore-S/wish their S/woosh-Fest
      It is their Well-nests & Whole-nests for Which we Wish
        . . . S/whirling S/wishing S/wells . . .
Swooping into Umoja Arms of Trust! Hushed in Imani Charms
  of Touch!
      . . . Meshing Akilah-Mo' & Mo'-Kilah . . .
Soul-plated/Soul-mated/Soul-fated: Tree-Steep'd Fruits . . .
      Southern-Ripened Sacto-Roots! Wish . . .
      S/whirl . . . S/whishhhhhhh . . .

Note: EBR is godfather of the bride, daughter of Ike & Jewel Paggett,
retirees from Sacramento's art & professional worlds circa mid-
2000s. They now live in Atlanta.)

Gwensways

for Gwendolyn Brooks, 1987

Cautious & Incantatory
Proverbial & Incremental
Kinetic & Incendiary

    She Languages down
        Un-illuminated
        Avenues
        Of The inflated
        The sleepwoke
        The impish   The august   The possessed
        The disengaged   The emblematic The ugly

Wearing her—
        make you wanna hiss/make you wanna hush
—verbal amulets
Like crosses;

    Pith
    Parchment and
    Prophecy
Fly from this intersperser of Dread-Words;

    O, the ways of our
    Wise counterclock woman!

Momenting the Ancestrail:
    Evocative, uneclipsed, evangelical:

    Intricate: Intimate:
    Her *Call*/Our *Response*
    Continuum.

Who were Those?

A poetic review of Clyde R. Taylor's *The Mask of Art:
Breaking the Aesthetic Contract*—film and literature
(on the occasion of his receiving the American Book Award)

at the moment of
masking, his vision triples:
20/20/20

Now a deep-see navigator
cogent clyde excavates the identity of the masked men
who abduct indigenous centuries & enter them
        in the colonial commissioners' log books
who encumber ancestral oeuvres in the name
        of cultural robber barons
who remove our mothers' lodes to alien
        museums of postminstrel history

*at the moment of
masking & mummifying
he dances with jazzombies*

This hipsofical priest
        rakish & bookish
of wholenest & conch/us/nest
performing a wedding
of sister viscera
& brother cerebrum

*he sees in circles—
"life through death upon these shores" with hayden—
contracts, expands, loves*

Whose gaze is steep as sterling brown's
(& glints like etheridge knight's
      locked-down sage who "sees thru stone")
& draws the unmasked men's naked faces
into the third whirl of brilliant babble

    achebe's arrow
    swings low: clyde saddles it &
    threads dumas' 3-ring ankh

& sews a mosaic a manifesto-in-progress
of everyblood's genesis & diaspora,
our moorings: fresh, yo, & ancestral

    (re: minutes from a meeting of the east saint african section of the
    clyde r. taylor booster club)

The Arched Bishop of New Art

for Amiri Baraka—In futuriam

I
Proletariat pontif—

His blackfulness
His wholeness

His bopness
His esthetic-efficient exactness

His hipness
His high frequency/Fahrenheit coolness

His down/ness   outlandishness
His jiveness   expoobidence

His brashness & his badness, i.e., full-up flame
Buttressed by the quick eyes of the daggerfire

Balancing bloods and Marx   making marks of his own

Lurking for the illusive
The black led-less
The lumpen/humpin bourgeoisie

II
Breakpoet of the pivot the pony the shuffle
The bootygreen & rim shot:

tack-a-map
tack-a-map
tack-a-map

Home-boy & hydra-tongued bard of the Blue Roi

Verb-pugilist in the service of the peoplehood:
When the poem calls
He comes out throwing
Antiphonal combinations
Lyrical lefts & rights
Rhythmical noun-jabs
His lores in the folkweighs
This finesser of rime & mime

        III

Retractor of doom   gnome-flirter   dismantler of occults
Divinator:
     'I See Yo Hi C'
     Said the Dark Gree Gree—

Who heals the uglylanguage;
Unfurls aphorisms and unwigs deceivers

A mass/man prevailing
Arched bishop of his ambivalence:
Worshipping deities of the dirty diction &
Practicing the art of prettyfication:

Wit-conjurer, who wordlessly converts
with the warm arms of consciousness—

Speaking to an anxious & enduring
Moment known as the multitude: a.k.a. people alias worker

Five'll get you some jive
Skin'll get you some kin*

or: caint the bishop burn?

A 75-line (prefatory) portrait of the poet as a life-long rebel

for Amiri, again, on his 75th birthday

hip cat-o-9-lives,
flipped every-which-a-way, lights
all-ways on his feet

yugen floats like a bear
& stings like spiced tea:
its winged poem kisses air
then falls into the black sea

marx's marks
sent him to cuba's cumbaya
&, after a six-pac,
to Sixth Pac

dreamed in volumes,
tiptoed thru daughter's thoughts,
fathering pomes, rebellions

found dante in the subway
among umpteenth circles
& jazz divinities

on the edge where whole life cuts,
bleeds hymns, him arts, him guts

the rage, off the page,
begets sage-roi, black kenning,
kinetic

heard devils' gospel
according to malcolm &
miles, hitching a ride
on the indigo's side
with duke's caravan

arched, like a bishop of new art,
he launched low fives from high heart

in '67 dame dunham said: "let's shake up east saint like dice:
bring in poet jones who'll move 'em like light scurries mice"

in east boogie's lincoln park, circa '69,
newark blue bard & simbas shine!

meanwhile kawaida embraced bright simbas on high street

he panned the neo-african way,
wrighted, rolled it
like lovers in hay

demon, denominator
of common lode
folk code
funk mode
priest & nommo chiseller—all explode

behind sublime or jody grind
he fire-loaded rhymes, back-loaded minds

pealed, peeled & repealed masks
with larry neal, he blackened tasks

Milestone: The Birth of an Ancestor

for Miles Dewey Davis, III
In Memoriam, In Futuriam
1926-1991

Prologue

Dressed up in pain
the flatted-fifth began its funereal climb
up the tribal stairwell:

grief-radiant as it
bulged and gleamed with moans
spread like laughter or Ethiopia's wings
mourned its own percussive rise
became blues-borne
in the hoarse East Saint Louis air

bore witness to the roaring calm
the garrulous silence
the caskets of tears
the gushing stillness:

the death of the Cool
became the birth of an Ancestor.

I

Cinematic tones cruised
the labyrinths of his youth:
he imbibed the bounciness of things,
treated himself to large helpings
of the cultural kaleidoscope,
forged from Africa, Armenia, Germany,
Poland; blurred by jazz, marbles,
Sousa, blues, Crispus Attucks, griots
grinding out 1917 riot-tales, boxing,

slingshots, spitballs, nightriders,
baseball, dice games, horseback
and poolsharks.

II

Code blue—10th Street
Code bop—Goose Hill and Broadway
Code cool—Lincoln High
Code hip—Harlem
Code hard-drive—Millstadt and Monterey
Code women—East St. Louis, Paris, the World

III

In the barbecue county of his youth,
he roamed the streets and alleys of snootville,
hung out on the gutbucket corners
      smelled the pungent yawn of stockyards
      heard the slaughtering drone of packinghouses
endured the endless river hours
coaxed horse-dawn dreams across
street-littered lives and
      antiseptic Sundays
with their rhythm-cradled heavens.

IV

O islands of jazz!
O peninsulas of opulence!
O glaciers of gold!
O trumpets of ice!
O floating barracoons of black pain!
O speeding blitz of sound!
O gaudy sufferings and abusive delights!

V

Life moved like film strips, quick
flick-like tones: cyclical, sonorous,
crowded with exits, one-way loves,

man-planned, prophetic, father-wise,
mortal, grooves of intravenous blues:
His sound the label of his Age: A Milestone.

VI

His music a marriage of cosmic trances
and funk-induced tremors: descended
from cavernous and oracular scrolls,
our collective heritages whispered
through his horn-loin of plenty:
honey silk moans lacing
race-riddled chapters of history.

But he would not be betrayed
by lingering barricades of color:
Milestone: his sound labeled his age.

VII

Labeled his Age? How so?
Hush-mouthed memories, kitchen-private,
churned up low, lusty acoustics draped
in Jack Johnson flamboyance:
tack-clean, pin-sharp, his conch/us
ears heard, relayed elegant and
elegiac inventories: Clifford, Lunceford,
Eric, Billie, Duke, Count, Thelonious,
Jimmy's fire this time, Sarah, Red Bonner,
Elwood Buchanan

VIII

Ghost-close, an ancestry of callings
opened him up to music-sweet thunder:
a symphony experimental and imagistic,
where dreamy jam sessions—delicate
vulnerable delirious—beckoned him
from the demon-cooled distances:
The heady swirl and princely snarl

of train tracks, sound tracks and needle tracks;
reminiscent rhythms eddying *Autumn Leaves*
or *If I Were a Bell I'd Be Ringing*
'bout *All Blues*, T*utu-Freedom*,
Water Babies churning out *Bitches Brew*
In a Silent Way and making *Sketches of Spain*.

Knowing that *Someday, Someday*,
their *Prince Will Come*. *Milestone*:
Sound that labeled an Age.

So, Yo! Home-Boy, Blues-Prince, Jazz-Pontif!
A mournful flag of release draped
over that hushed horn of plenty:
yet brilliant rumblings start up again
as this native son goes marching in;
brilliant rumblings spreading
like laughter or Ethiopia's wings,
mourning their own percussive rise,
becoming blues-borne above
the hoarse East Saint Louis air:
bearing witness to the roaring calm
the garrulous silence
the caskets of ears
the gushing stillness:
from the Death-ash of the Cool-flame
comes the Warming Birth of an Ancestor.

Mandela's Home Where the Ancient Word Walks

I
Sightings

Nelson Mandela is plural, *toyi toyi!*,
Innumerable, a totem
Of multiplications: vertical,
Horizontal, mythical. He swells,
Has range and eclipse, as in mountainous.
Marked *fragile* now, he endures like
Vintage as dignified cynosure of grapevine,
Drum, phone, kalimba, newsprint, TV, kora.
   toyi toyi!

II
Drink of Release Drink of Disaster

Yet, for breath-drenched me,
Balanced six-floors up above grey Detroit,
The Canadian border nodding at my back,
Worming word of his day came via touch-tone
& digit: Loretta Dumas's intonating reminder:
"Nelson Mandela's on all three networks!"

III
An Ancient Man; The Long Weight

There is righteousness in an ancient man's walk:
Mandela walking and whistling our torrid fears.
Amandla endlessly astride circles,
Mandela stalking squares,
Amandla traversing rectangles—
For 27 years—but never walking

Perpendicular to jealous struggle.
>*toyi toyi!*

Nevermind occasional, oblique
Streams of stray torments, arrayed
Within racially-wrought identity frames.
Nor the guilt-edged glee of puppet-dynasties.

IV

Depth/Throng: Mandela Plan

For 27 years, Bantu, Panther, Mau Mau
Muslim, Zulu, Exile, Xhosa and a hundred
Hungering diasporas held their breaths.
Awaiting release of Deepthrong son: Even
Mothers, heaving up their centuries of prayers,
Shrugged and by-passed their own hearts
For this 27-year trek to the Shrine of Patience.
O how they grinned and bore an ugly
Government ulcerous with detour signs.

V
>*toyi toyi!*

A hundred hungering diasporas jettisoned
South Africa, South Carolina and South
Chicago, until their silent clamors
Conjured Mandela up from his electric
Asylum: Father-confessor for the masked
Media who watch an ancient man walking:
Child-elder, spite-shined, mobile-erectus-obelisk,
Quantum-fetish, accessing the lonely
Stool, inhaling the 27-year-old Soweto Sigh,
Warm-eyed sabre, whose moon-glint messages
A *toyi toyi* Nation, recoiling, embryonic,
>Imminent.

Mandela plural & mythic: 27 sleepless years
Treading air, parrying freak squads,
Re-ordering stars, scaling altars of exercise,
Spearing dreams, lapping the "luminous dark,"
Doing the *toyi toyi*, Walking the watch.

Labored for Maya (October 11, 1991)

Blues-Ode for the Foredreamers

For Willie Epps, on the occasion of his retirement

His foredreamers saddled the centuries like see-saws
        & rode ancestrails—through kingdoms & villages—
across the bone-paved Middle Passage
        into the embrace of thrones and shackles

then—like Mandinka & Mississippi bowmen—
        he sighted in on Douglass's North Star
& used Cahokia or Kentucky windage
        to snare the long-shot-of-a-Prize
in the cross-hairs of hope

hurdling plantation, cave, railroad track & swamp
he played the river's moods like a guitar:
climbed its banks like Buffalo Soldiers,
his flickering dreams burning full-up

as weaver & bobber in the Second Middle Passage
        —a child of ArkanSippi—
he was tattooed for life:
        a thought called East St. Louis
bluesplendent in its moans
        etched itself into each island of his brain

in Milesville & Jackie's Junction & Dunham's Diaspora
his flickering dreams sizzled full-up like jazz
rising, reprising Africa & high-fiving history!

        "East Saint ain't dead yet!" the drumcestors crooned,
"&Willie . . . He's got the scars and tattoos to prove it!"

Daughter

Treasure translates
        voices s-c-r-a-w-l-e-d between
   the warring zones
  of   my   life

    mines the ore of marginalia
  stored in the cuffs of her memory
      re-w/raps it in acoustical carvings
from the drumwalls of nzinga's africa

   young
              gifted
   & stacked
she pantomimes hyperbolic love
for her mother elsie while keeping
   a
   third
   eye
on her father's periphery/centers:

   figures that gnawing on
   me is knowing herself

Haiku

honeyfunk

sugarsisterspice
twice-swarming wine's honeyfunk:
baptism in blue

shay   shay

blues/sheroes shay shay
along war-roads of giants,
girlcentered dreams trailing

star-rider

wear the world's skin,
o star-rider, jazz scented
in bodysuits of eros

singing in green

Daisy O. Wesbrook's
ensemble masks blisters, rings
all-mighty: God sings Green

cornrows ripple

cornrow-proud wishes
ripple across bareheaded
dreams: girlwomen rise!

sweet dangers

pain-bright exemplars
—Scotia, Maya, Oprah, Jackie—
danger-sweetened triumph

memwars

unfolded fingers—
palm-shores cradling nations—
life-lines to memwars

jump-starter

woman jump-starting
worlds: dawns, midwiferies, moons
yestermorrow's junes

honeyfunk #2
(Tanka)

bopping the hiphopisms
jazzing the "be" of your 3rd eye
soularkestrally
twice-warming wine's honeyfunk
twice-honeyfunking the wine

foxgoddess

foxgoddess straddled
hell's heart : icy bronco-queen
taming juice-hot flames

Wyvetter: The Navigator & Elevator

for the late Honorable Wyvetter Hoover Younge,
1930-2009

O Crown Jewel of People Renewal . . .

Buoyed by her 1940's vow—
to navigate & elevate East Saint Love—
& pondering future decades of collaboration
with Katherine Dunham & R. Bucksminister Fuller,
our Precocious Joan of Arc reached genius-level marks
while her generation of marchers & academic archers
braved the World's Second War
& Ole Jim Crow's lynch-hot tar.

Our Jewel in the Crown of People Renewal . . .

Her beloved Lincoln High School tooled
line after line of educator & artist, physician & athlete,
jazzician & minister, social leader & businessman . . .
And Wyvetter went on a-blazin' & a-bloomin'
into a wizard of jurisprudence that would,
like Billie Jones & Thurgood Marshall,
floor the color bar & stretch-stretch far-far,
like a vigilant search engine, into any
crevice or noose of social abuse
(& dislodge it like a surgeon).

People Renewal Was Her Crown Jewel . . .

Our s/hero applied her young legal plow
to turn over two-faced fields of injustice
& raise her people's pow-wow powers
(with self-reliant town hall hours)
where they plotted new dreamscapes, lovescapes &
familyscapes,
& became Richer Jewels of Human Renewal.

Jump-starting us in the mid-20th Century,
like a 21st Sentry Barack Hussein Obama,
Wyvetter's life-length paradigm
was a songified & souljahfied rhyme
—that echoed Nzinga's & Zora's choruses
& Mary Bethune's & Nina's warrior-tunes
—plus a precursor of model & mentor
molded from her high-tech intellect.

The Crown Jewel in the Tiara atop the
Variegated Garden of People Renewal . . .
now hovers above the Forest of East Saint Love:
The Crown Jewel of People Renewal . . .

Carolyn, our Mandolin . . . like Gwendolyn

for Carolyn Marie Rodgers, 1940–2010

jumping bad meant jumping phine thru rites
of hoop-lined passage: street corner simfony,
storied kitchen operas, sashay ballets, lightly or
deeply read tales trailin' the wakeful ntu
wake-less-nests of night where, in
Senghor's words, image meets rhythm, making you
& I poets before self-knowing dawn/s . . .

from unknown dreamer-rhymer to Black Bird
gifted with gloved talons 2 get us
ovah: like Roberta's soft-stingin' stanzas, you
ferry posses of umoja-lovers thru straits
of the soul-deaden'd & self-slain.
Seeking encore, we hear ayibobo's echo behind
your final soulo, our ovation in your words

SECTION NINE
Kwansabas
1990s to 2012

EBR, flanked by Loretta Dumas (L, widow of Henry Dumas) and
Margaret Walker Alexander (R). Medgar Evers College. 1988.

A Note on the Origin of the Kwansaba

(adapted from an essay that appeared in the 2004 issue of *Drumvoices Revue*)

Hindsight suggests that inventing the "kwansaba" in 1995—in East Saint Louis, Illinois—was not only appropriate but fortuitous. At that time, the nine-year-old Eugene B. Redmond Writers Club—organized/chartered in March 1986 by a group of cultural workers and creative artists that included Sherman L. Fowler and Darlene Roy—was searching for new tools, concepts, vehicles, and challenges within regional and global contexts. The kwansaba emerged from our early practice of reconfiguring Dr. Maulana Karenga's seven-day Kwanzaa holiday to fit our one-day Pre-Kwanzaa Ritual—staged on the third Tuesday of December. Folding a seven-day Kwanzaa celebration into a two-hour free family event, including a procession of our Soular Systems Ensemble and Sylvester "Sunshine" Lee's Community Performance Ensemble, became what I call a "choreo-musico-poetic-mosaic." Our ritual flowed around the Nguzo Saba (Seven Principles), using the candle-lighting feature as the colorful and dramatic core.

Over several months I toyed with the Swahili words "Kwanzaa" (First Fruits) and "Saba" (Principles) until the term "kwansaba" hit me like fresh—or ancestral—love. A poem consisting of seven lines, of seven words each, with no word containing more than seven letters,* this original form was then correlated with a recitation of each of the Nguzo Saba (Seven Principles): Umoja, Kujichagulia, Ujamaa, Ujima, Kuumba, Nia, Imani. Assigned kwansabas were hammered out in offices, classrooms, basements, dens, cars, bedrooms, kitchens, living rooms, or bathrooms and brought to our twice-monthly meetings for critiques.

Fleshing out the concept for the kwansaba also required all manner of other extra-literary leaps, if you will, into astronomy, astrology, numerology, and mythology—all based

---

*Exceptions to the seven letter rule are proper nouns, foreign terms, and quoted passages.

on/in the Arabic numeral 7. Henry Lee Dumas (1934-1968), "patron saint" of EBR Writers Club, was my creative muse in the general incubation process that led to the creation not only of the "kwansaba" but Black River Writers Press (1968).

As readers will note, I never hesitate to speak of Dance Doyenne Katherine Dunham's influence on our writing circles in East St. Louis. While Madame Dunham had no direct hand in the creation of this new poetic form, her momentous arrival in our city (1967) at the height of the Black Arts Movement and one year after the invention of Kwanzaa, was a catalyst for both general and specific revolutions in cultural arts, social/political thought, and community service. The Dunham "Legacy" has influenced many of us in very identifiable ways. For example, some poets and dancers have studied the Dunham Technique, while others have written scholarly papers or poems (in other forms) about her. Thirty-six years ago, Sherman Fowler and I served as consultants to Miss Dunham at her Performing Arts Training Center and are among hundreds of her "sons" in East St. Louis. A tribute collection of *Drumvoices*, "Kwansabas for Katherine," included veteran poets like Amiri Baraka (who contributed a "copacetic" non-kwansaba), Shirley LeFlore (offering a near-kwansaba), and Tyrone Williams; first-time kwansaba-carvers and new Dunham aficionados; and, along the corridor in between, some exciting experimenters—all being sharpened on anvils and leg-acies of precision a la Madame Dunham's example.

Sankofa Kwansaba for Reginald Lockett
1947–2007

panther, poet & good-footer, could songify
like a word-wind ballad dear. enters
yester-morrow's funky far evers, wearing peace
epaulet over war-tested grace. leaning like
love's hit man into born again ears
of a jazz convert. blowin' on the
corner of West Oakland & West Africa.

Two Kwansabas for Patrick Teye Narter, World Patriot & Patriarch

1926-2013

I

O Omni-Present One: Thanks for gifting
Gloria & Patrick—each-to-each—so
Sweetly, to tour each other's soul's stroll.
And thanks, Gloria, our aria, for gifting
Us with Patrick—world-fluent Sankofa man—
Design'd by his Supreme Maker not as
A taker, but a waker of lives.

II

We are more wakeful, thanks to Patrick
And his faith-laced glow, center'd knowing,
Astute global-family rites of passage via
His Ghana, his Germany, his Denmark, his
America, his Somerset, his mindset/love-set
And, now, his sunset—re-rising from ancestrails,
Waking us to more bright yester-morrows.

Upbringing: The Pedagogy of East Boogie*
Three Kwansabas

#1 Grandmother's Soulversity

whether churnin' lye into soap, earth into
produce, clabber into butter, sass into whippin,
snow into ice cream, sermon into succor,
hair into plait, body-ash into glisten,
theory into thimble, remnant into quilt, kitchen
into sparkle—or what-not into feast—
her edict was, "get some learnin', boy."

#2 School of Weavin' & Bobbin'

every boy/girl a garden of dreams:
croonin' like Nat Cole, Eckstine, Johnny Ace;
chirpin'/beltin' like Billie, Ella, Big Mama;
bobbin'/jabbin' like Brown Bomber; slinkin' silkily
like Eartha & Katherine; coppin' cool like
Miles; swingin' low like dues howlin' 'neath
Wolf's blues, like grandma's chariot—home-gone.

#3 Academy of Low Heights

swingin' low—fetchin' sky; saddlin' moanin' noon's
evening sun; ark-eye-texts of black
studies ridin' hair trigger of double-being
into an all-night palaver & hearin'
blood-shot sages scream, "we're schizophrenics with
split personalities!"; mountin' new *courses*—ala Olaudah,
Sojourner & Malcolm—back to East Boogie

*Nickname for East St. Louis, Illinois

Local "Sun" Was Central to "Black Dance-USA"

East St. Louis' own Sylvester ("Sun"-shine) Lee and his Community Performance Ensemble launched Better Family Life's star-spangled "Black Dance-USA: A Celebration in Movement." Held at Washington University's Edison Theatre on May 23, 2009, the concert, themed "Harmattan: The Winds of Change," also featured "Spirit of Angela" and "MaTiff Hip-Hop" dance companies."

Suffusing the night with "conch/us/nest"-raising art, performers extolled cultural traditions—and the need to save our planet ("house-whole")—through scintillating choreography, drums of fire and drama. All garnished with enlightening narration by BFL's Malik and DeBorah Ahmed. Homage via kwansabas follows . . .

Dancin' Thru Fresh & Ancestral Passages

Bellies & limbs groove under squirm-throbs
of bald-headed-beaded drums that murmur,
gallop & clap like thunder, shaping a
freshly-ancient metro from energy-waves of
gele & djembe, shakere & kente, boom-
barrel & plie, goom-boppin' hey-hey:
spiced with calabash, buba, agbada & sashay!

Xplodin' off the stage's hollow dark-nests,
Sunshine's hallow'd drum bodies, a-wash in
ageless cones of light—while worryin' ears
& eyes like one-hundred-proof blues—
link Mother Earth's honored family rites with
birth-sweatin' *Spirit/s of Angela* in a
dervish-whirlin' Harmattan of tough love-scapes.

Now jerkin'/flailin' amid hectic urban horrors
that pollute Soular Systems, motors of *MaTiff
Hop* board a *s/Hip* sailing stages of word-
less speech called DANCE: saddlin' bright night
mares, they ride ghetto-glyphic waves of
earthly & astral beauty—these marvels of
culture—into Queen Dunham's Obama-Era Village.

Hey, Hey, L J is OK

for Dr. Lena J. Weathers on her 80th Birthday, 2010

East Saint's Brainy Beauty & bobby-soxed
Lincoln Knight's awash in the Forties, drools
over books, drama & court ship at
Fisk, prepping to Weather (with an "s")
Fifties *cum* Sixties' storms & more decades
of day-breaks, a.k.a. losses, wins, draws
& a sixfold bundle of jubilee, OKAY!

South by West by World

A kwansaba for sister/colleague
Hortense Simmons, 2010

like delta blues hitchin' trains headin' upSouth,
Florida ferries you to Howard/Ohio/California—
Sacto, to be exact-o!—spinnin' webs of
leader, scholar, lover & future from the
mean & cream of academe: amidst which
you, esteem'd college teacher at sea—flava'd
& FREE, elope with a Florida dream.

Break Word with the World

In East Saint Love & 12 other
urban orbs we break silence & words
with Ishmael Reed & PEN Oakland's watch
keepers who yearly enlist third eye soul-
scopes in vigils to shield the dissed
& unloved with razor-edge verbs &
nouns: arms for the fallen—& risen.

Fun & "Conch/Us/Nest" at ESL'S "Earth Day"

Full of good times and "conch/us/nest," East Saint Love's "Earth Day" celebration, sponsored by the Wyvetter H. Younge Center for Economic and Social Justice (of the Mary Brown Center), got underway on Saturday, April 25, 2009, in historic Lincoln Park.

Known as "ritual" ground—touched by "greats" like John Kirkpatrick, Malcolm X, Roy Campanella, Barbara Ann Teer, Miles Davis, Jackie Joyner-Kersee, Amiri Baraka, Katherine Dunham, Taylor Jones III, Clyde C. Jordan, and Stokely Carmichael—the park was a "familistic" scene of food, tree-planting, games, prizes, poetry, music, vendors' booths, service agency tables, speeches, and citizens from all walks of life. The following "kwansabas" render the day poetically.

Earth Day in East Saint Love

East Saint Love, Cousin Earth & Sun
"embrace" / "rejoice" on a hopin-hoppin Day
of 2-gather-nests: tots-teens-adults
jumpin', dancin', hot-doggin' in Lincoln Park's
family house-whole, swingin' in poet-trees
with sister keepers & a laureate . . . Elders'
whisper-rings of pride swellin' like steam

Hearty homage to Her Honor Wyvetter H.
Younge from our hue-man love-hive:
Between slice of sky & rich floor
of kin-life, we stretch like a
grandma-blanket or Edna Patterson-Petty quilt.
See how their loving patches map DNA
from Mother Africa to East Saint Arkansippi.

East Coast Tapestry Kwansaba

holla—subway storms—Harlem to Key West,
haul jazz n pizza, beans n salsa,
Apollo nights & writers rites, medals for
Maya & Amiri, [synergy-furious] bardic flowers
in Philly, New Ark, DC & Virginia
showers. Saddle Atlanta's festive heights & Miami's
Asili (Cuban-Haitian & Book Fair) sights.

The Gather-Rings Kwansaba

clappin' or claspin' in kindred coves, slippin'
into or raisin' spirit/s, Maya will songify
gather-rings, riffin'soulo—or choral—on
life's heights. Rife with nia, she'll sweeten
a bitter tale in a suite of
good foots flatted by elegant ham bones
on a bed of rice next to blues soufflé.

Maya's Birthdaze Kwansaba

Who can snap a finger like Maya—
& have our chests swell open like
Sesame? In the Caribbean Sea, beached among
Palms in Florida or California (with Oprah's
"Legends"), on Reynolds' Winston-Salem "island," vista
& vintage spread like wine & music
—& bows of raining roses. Snap, cameras!

kwansaba: yo maya! yo day!

bible cats, the bard, dunbar, jimmy &
us—o song-borne sister—sittin' pretty
with ailey at the bar/re: sippin' on
sugar-flaked after-calls in a twilite
of memwars masked as poetry—in a
whirl of diz, wiz, love biz, viz:
rainbow holler-rings: yo' maya! yo' day!

Maya's Sun Rides Waves

Horror's twin is Joy! So knows Maya:
proxy-mating heart quakes, jivin' still-rising
word zeal, whirlin down whirl's sun-ways
like a blues-aged angel-moon, stylin'
real/reelin' in bardic soulos—as Proud
Oprah accepts baton of she-pomes &
Maya laughs in the Key of !Thunder.

Mood Maya Kwansaba

she feeds eyes, ears & skies with
dancing loaves of poetry—baked in aware
nests of Stamps, St. Louis, San Francisco
& *Porgy and Bess*—then, fore-tasting
purple Alice (s) & blue Toni (s), she uncages
Dunbar's lyrical feasts in Nasser's Egypt, Nkrumah's
Ghana, MLK's USA & Every Woman's Kitchen.

Kwansaba Tales Tall as Maya

"You want to know how it feels
to give birth, my dear brother? Imagine
pulling your upper lip over your head
like a stockin' cap." . . . Mid-80s/church-
theater & Maya's serving slices of Winston-
Salem/house-talk to me & the
Sister-ring: Ruth Love & Dolly McPherson . . .

raising an after-repast glass we share
a mid-70s memwar from Sonoma (California)
Wine Country: Second Brother Jimmy Baldwin's Paris-
borne/e epistle: "writing is like shitting bricks."
Then an Africa-aged pause, quake-filled
—& quiet—as a poem's pounce, as
a San Andreas or New Madrid Fault . . .

Lookingback: Jazzstained Jayne: 3 Kwansabas

for Jayne Cortez, 1934-2012

Circa sixty-nine: after poetin out a
November ice/mare at Buffalo's Inter-American
Writers Congress (with Robert Hayden, Ishmael Reed
& Stanley Crouch), Quincy Troupe & I,
like gung-ho GI's, climbed jazz-stained stairs
where eyes/ears met an edible montage
above Big Apple's Avenue of the Americas . . .

Ornate in its oblique nest, like Ornette's
lofty funk/scapes, Jayne's 4th floor walk-
up earth-whiled into archive, studio, sanctum,
repast, poem: sister-threads winding festivals &
funerals thru joyful/elegiac mazes: exiting from
penises & pearl tongues of artful exults,
in magic/reel yawps of yari yari . . .

Now, Jayne's axe-bright tomes, flashin &
spittin torrent thru turrets of her fecund
decades, grieve & sculpt a pell mel/l,
you know, of AIDS, female spill/age,
drug gorge/s, walking-dead peeps, impish pimples
on a carcass dressed up in money,
Tranes blowin, rollin too soon into gone . . .

Three Kwansabas for Homegirl Barbara Ann's Harlem Homegoing

You entered East Saint Love in 1937,
jump street's "Action Arts" baby, ridin' a
streak of gray hair that Mother Lila
said meant wealth: now, wearing purple &
white, mourner & reveler, drawn—like you
—by horse, drummer, chanter & horn blower,
"possess" Harlem's flesh-, brick- & glass-scape.

Outside Riverside Church, an elegant elephant
greets you: dove & balloon release you.
But not your East Saint African Leg-a-sea:
a soul-trust of priests, Avery Brooks,
Lythcotts Omi & Sade ("little Bobbi"), Faisons
& Samuels, warbler-goddess Roberta Flack, Ruby
Dee, Woodie King, Amiri & Sonia, dancing . . .

Arcs of Alvin Ailey's agile arks, gracing
mazes of air in limb & song . . .
Glenn Turman & Robert Hooks—the latter
by letter thru Hattie Winston—letting in
light you rode to s/teer lost loves,
from self-hatred's glowing magnets of deceit,
back ntu arms of East Saint Harlem.

*Founder of National Black Theater in 1968: East Saint Louis Native
Daughter Barbara Ann Teer (1937-2008) Was Sent "Home" by Hundreds of
Mourners & Revelers in Harlem (July 27, 2008)*

Margaret's Salon of Good Luck & Trouble

up-north Sister 'Sippi's subway-deep in
new bones & neck bones—& neck
n neck with high-rise jazz, low-
ridin' salsa & soul-loded shout-outs
to blue Lou. locked in Medusa-dreads,
she can conjure Kush, cotton fields, Timbuctoo
& barbecue, Port au Prince & Quince.

a-whirl-whirl in our merry-migrant
world of good luck & trouble, Sister
'Sippi samples the Big Apple, then, as
Califia girl, surfs La Jolla's pearls before
u-turning to Harlem & troupin' islands
of Ellington, Bird Land, Ella & Ellison. Loopin'
Guadeloupe, she opens a whole gold heart.

in all seasons, she seasons her Salon
with peas & teas, vases & *vases,*
spices & ices & tooth-sweet vices,
pots, pans & potted plants in exotic
hands, cacti & rock & rye, studio
arts & after-scarf tarts, rum-dreamt
laugh downs & belly-royal humor unbound.

roundin' the sundial of a whole 'nother
decade she slaps fifty-nine high-fives,
then high-lifes with Fela & Masekela,
sashays with a sky scraper named Porter,
bikes thru Central Park under a hung-
over moon, tastes mestizo-gumbo at Flor
de Mayo & Saint Blues ju-doo, *solid.*

Oprah at 55

five on the five-five side, O,
to start this Windy City flo-show
where Zora has eyes for Tea Cake
& ruby Ruby cures Ossie's heart ache;
Q escorts Alice down Purple lane as
Gayle, Toni & Maya eye Beloved's main
man: Barack glowin' like a White House clock.

Kwansaba for Sheryl's Pilgrimage

for Sheryl Yvette Johnson, 1955–2007

Hers was a pilgrim age to narrate
a page or orate a stage or
create a sage starred with kush-filled
airs & heirs of Hetshepsut—Sheryl's nom
de plume!—hajj that became her bardic
leg-a-sea, her diva-vine: stretch,
O statue-as-queen—who wholes us.

A Troupe of Kwansabas
For a Bloodsman of Tropes

So what's blood worth to you, Quincy?
Watts of jagged images that main-line
veins of your canvas like ritual-dancin',
bling-slung zombies? High-fivin', low-jivin'
homeys boardin' juju's of conch-us-nests
while you songify river skulls & ocean
hulls—& ask, *Hoo wants to gno?*

How blood be, QT? A vamp re:
vessels of styles ala Satchmo & Miles?
Kindred saints chuck-walkin' ntu doo-wop?
Ellison's blues-maze to end visible angst?
Or Ish's sync-phonic Legba/ba liturgy? So
what, if Jimmy's straits filter Marquez &
Morrison thru Dumas' ankh—with no chaser?

Poets, jazzers & rebels ain't orphans: just
pariahs in the wheres of some: but
blood keeps boardin' express Tranes to mothers,
muses & Cherokee Lovers; flyin' Jubas &
Daedaluses back to myth nests, hippin' to
catch hops between sacred tomes & flatted
pomes that shay shay with vévé—dig?

Arkansippi (Midwest) Kwansaba

Ankh Dumas helps rivers of lazy-fury
dream them-selves back to Ra's design:
enroute they sculpt scapes of [windy] cities,
hamlets, skies; echo ear trails: riot of
seven-teen, Joplin's meanest swings, bop's KC
kings, boogaloo's gut-strings, hiphop's eye-'coustic
blings: festive waves awaitin' ice-conked winters.

A Triptych of Kwansabas for a Triptych of Bodies & Souls

After Lucian Krukowski's "Danae—After Titian"

I

A *Renaissance* dawns again in these musings.
On art's altar, altered sites of artist
& viewer, divine/d by magic's & moment's
charred coal, are birthed in swirlin' wombs
of lights. While shades of darks host
swollen curves in their quiet swoosh/swoop/
swishin peek-a-boos with Lord Zeus.

II

Time's Sum's drawn in anthro-choreo-motifs:
psycho-soular-glyphic lines, wholes halved, reduced,
recast, oft-cumber'd by cubes of thought,
deus-ragged & nommo-jazzed in labored
visions of *danae*, stitch, stroke, lore, doubt.
Though Zeus's where-a-bouts are any
zealot's or god's guess: get me Lucian?

III

Solve for logic or Solve for art.
Or: twice-tart 40-year junkets in
hearts of Big Apple & Saint Lou.
Just don't devolve to lower you's by
sapping credo's muse. Art is soul's gold,
booty enrich'd in a den's visual din
of trill, thresh, winnow, brush of tongue.

A Bouquet of Kwansabas

Dunham's 2 Souljourns to East Saint Earth

Paris-borne by the mid-20s, Josephine
Baker had fled mid-west hunger &
riot when mid-teen Katherine soul-sassed
from Chicago, samplin' East Saint Love, Alton
—amidst Miles' birth year—& blue Saint
Loo. Later, global rites of stage-glow
lit Miss D's mid-60's re-entry . . . "ayíbobo!"

Dunham Omen

Omen-hips swivel from girl to woman
world, then hurdle a mind-wide village
of drum-fluent lovers cooing like amulets
of blues 'round her ninety-six-year-
old temple: with a diva's ease, she's
still swift as a samurai, wake-filled
dreamer, aye, eye-wide in fierce slumber.

Inferno Amiri

Cooler be baraka than bebop's inferno, sixties-
phat juke man doo-ing his hoo-downs
in sizzling laps of funk/spheres, hip
blaster of dreams ntu streams "cold" as
a trane rhymin rails & rinds, slaves'
left-behinds, bruised peeps, blues peeps, ark-
new/dirge-ditties in the collard section.

Third Cup & WSQ

His tangy guitar spices blue-noted/wee-
hour air: eddie fisher accepts hand-off
of leo gooden's *third cup*, hamiet bluiett
kisses a bare-toned brass conch, lifting
black artists group & world saxophone quartet
above malcolm-eyed cities: then, flight of
soundz: julius hemphill, oliver lake, david murray.

Melba & Dahveed

Drum-tongue'd poetree sprouts from *obsidian* earth:
Motor City Melba & Detroit Dahveed, *feeling*
thru forests of Hughes' doo-w/operas, link
Dudley, Naomi, Marvin, Woodie, Ron, Stevie, Re-Re,
commute between Pair-a-dice Valleys &
East Boogie's BAM rallies, genius zooming genius,
yes Rosa, on Motown's Planet of Poets.

2 Margarets & Gwen

2 Margarets (burroughs/walker) & Gwen's Friend
Ship brook/s Harlem's wakeful 20s & Baraka's
he/arts-riffin' 60s: her-storied South Side
Arts Center '37, Yale Younger Poets award
'42, *Annie Allen's* Pulitzer '50, & a
brother/ring of Richard/Dudley/Hoyt—raisin'
DuSable, OBACee, Haki, maryemmagraham, black/whirl's
pearls . . .

Sonia's Phat Moon Blues

moon phat in soprano & Philly Dog,
Sonia moans Alabama babies in civil mournin,
worryin Sterling's lines—! O Langston's—! O Gwen's
—! O High John's—! O Delta rootress's—name-
callin ! Marie! Zora! Maya! Toni (s)! Alice ! Gloria
& molten-sweet! Malcolm-tongued epitome epitome
—! resist—sayen don't pity me, sayen ! resist . . .

Remi Raji

Remi's poem's window's what/how we'll see
Nigeria thru; Africa too; even America's in
Remi's vista's stew, *a poetic* guided *tour,*
as he titles one view, &, later,
ex-prez Bill arrives for rehab in
"Clinton's Song": Remi images world's ails in
yonders of rain/bow/blue/s—god's hue/s.

EBR Riders

As off-springs of cake walk, swing
& tornado alley—& heirs of riots
& floods—they agreed to write out
gulf storms of tonkin, persia & katrina-
rita—o fabled cradle of juju, juneteenth
& jazz!—these arkan-sippi bards bearin
aliases like blues, charlois, darlene, roscoe, sheryl . . .

Kwansaba Canvas & Coda for Gwen at 90
1917–2000

paint satin legs on phat bronze frame
defend us like smith & wesson, then
teach us to reclaim our ancient name
feed hungry poets with blues-minted notes
rite 99 words about Ankh Dumas' ghosts
amtrak to East Saint Love from Chicago
to gift us with Kwanzaa's ritual glow . . .

Gwen-Gwen, you opened jazz-hued gates,
hewed conch/us/nests from bardic straits:
as you ascend your 9th decade, seems
only yester morrow we made poetry's quilt:
80 lyrical patches to share your 80th:
so set sail/s—habara gani, ancestrails!

Written in 2007 on what would have been Gwendolyn Brooks's 90th birthday.

Miles Davis Arts Festival

East St. Louis, Illinois, 2001

Ablaze on Ahmad Jamal's River Front of
Rhythms, Russell Gunn & Oliver Sain, Herbie
Hancock & Wayne Shorter, Quincy Troupe &
Clark Terry, Erika Johnson & Phil Perry
gifted Deborah Granger's First Miles Fest. And
Nile-toned gods like Ra & Trane
sprayed rains & bows with "all blues."

Long Distance Prodigies Davis & Haynes

Jazzed by Duke Ellington's "East Saint Louis
Toodle-oo," boogie bottom licked tastes of 1917's
riot from its memory, scraped hate from
race-scorch'd soil & sent teenage sons—
trumpet-magi Miles & piano prodigy Eugene
Haynes—to Juilliard School of Music, after
first soulo voyages at Lincoln High School.

Dumas' Rebirth in Word-Deed

Awake as a quake, dreamin' Henry wrought
Hank into "Ankh," Duma into "Samud": named
his poems "sabas" & "ikefs," his friends
"Headeye" & "Jonoah," his settings "Sweetwater" &
"Harlem," his vessels "afro-horn" & "soul-
boat," his heroes "Probe" & "Sun Ra,"
& his brothers "Fon" & "cosmic arrows."

Kwansaba-Elegy for Atty. Richard G. Younge

You were a Defense that never rested,
Richard, an Umoja-def nest filled with
tillers of kindred earths & tenders of
weapons-grade rainbow-dreams that bred
toasts & sagas in people-storied fields. Now,
as in yester-century, your Nia-*briefs*
produce many morrows' harvest of warrior-hearts.

Fire-Wrought Wright (as in Richard)

half-slavery blue(s)-printed wright, hunger-spun
& flight-flung him, like a saddle, atop
nomadic north stars of douglass & marx.
with kindred neo-run-a-gates he
fore-shadow'd casts of migrant funk-villes:
sky-lines of s/low-risin' juke dreams,
holy daddies rolling in store-front grace

he hissed & laughed, plotted & penned
double-faced images of alien & native,
negro first & negro-phobe, boundin' from
chicago's bronze villes & suburbs to big
apple's sub-waves & rise-highs: then
paris' patriot parlors with their switch-bladed
ideo-blogs: geneses of coups, corps, nations

fire-wrought & buckled in verbs, he
swashed across pagan spain & Africa: miss
(sun-black) sippi's richard of hearths whose
avant vision-turned style beckon'd baldwin &
ellison, senghor & diop, sartre & de beavoir,
juju & haiku, yerby & etta moten:
moment's kinfok, all-wright, his & ours

Genesis' "Youth Arts" Event
"Dazzled" Audience
YOUNG & OLD ENJOYED EASTER CONCERT
STARRING JAZZ TITAN BENNY GOLSON

As attested to by the accompanying poems ("kwansabas"), Easter Sunday's "Youth in the Arts" Benefit Concert at St. Louis' Sheldon Memorial Auditorium was not only a SUCCESS—it dazzled! (The baton of Miles Davis, Clark Terry, May Wheeler, and Leon Thomas was indeed handed down!)

Featuring former East St. Louis Lincoln Senior High School Jazz Band Master Ron Carter, who was sandwiched between Delano Redmond's ESL Senior High School Jazzers and the renowned saxophonist-composer Benny Golson, the event—the 5th annual—was sponsored by Genesis Academy of Arts Ministry. Founder-Director of "Genesis" is Tracy D. Holliway-Wiggins.

Carter, who brought his Northern Illinois University Jazz Ensemble to town, produced award winning musicians and groups at Lincoln High—and at NIU—as has his former Lincoln student, Redmond, at East Side. Carter also co-authored a jazz textbook with his former student (now SIUE professor) Reginald Thomas and trumpet great cum musicologist Wynton Marsalis.

Golson, composer of brilliant and memorable works like "Whisper Not" and "Killer Joe," ranks alongside such geniuses of jazz as Duke Ellington and John Coltrane, with whom he once played. He has also composed music for television shows and big screen movies.

And the audience? Well, that's a whole 'nother memorable story: numerous standing ovations and spontaneous bursts of applause, lots of heads a-bobbing, shoulders & torsos a-snaking, and hips a-hopping.

Three Kwansabas for
Geniuses of 'Genesis' Jazz

East Side High "puts a pot on"

Jumpin' in a "pot," Delano's child jazzers
brew'd stew for Ron, Benny & kin.
Then, like hungry rivers & winds, their
gumbo of aromas rose to higher-glyphs—
tone-storied mosaics of blues-bop-cool,
joy anew in mouths-hands-fingers-feet,
seducin' both old & freshly minted ears.

Ron's Universal Swingers/Jammers

More gumbo stews in Lou's blues basin
as Ron filters Joplin, Handy, Miles, Fontella
& Leon Thomas: tastes of tonal hues,
brass streams, improv pop-ups, dap taps,
snares of moon light scats with ol'
hep cats and meadow larks in Vermont,
while other birds "didn't know about love."

Benny Golson: Genesis/Elder of Avant Garde

Sax's hissing, snaking, breath-lush dream reels
in memwars of 'Trane, Diz, Blakey, Horace:
then "Along Came Betty"—& Benny—on
a Broad-way-stroll with "Killer Joe"—
da-da da. Blow-man, Benny's horn a-plenty
beams like his sculpt'd fore-head: Cool,
we'll "Whisper Not" 'midst his "Blues March."

X-Ray

for Raymond Campbell, in memoriam

Raymond was awake even when asleep, a
real night metro gnome honing reel skills
thru lens of eye-magi-nation. Genius
of Tudor Avenue, big brain/big dreamin'/
big brother, aspired to be fired into
world-minds, awhirl in pools so idea-
steeped, he could become an x-Ray

Section Ten
"Da-Dum-Dun"
Memwars Of The 1960s
Black Arts Movement

EBR in the Henry L. Dumas Memorial Organic Garden.
Sweet Home, Arkansas (near Little Rock). 2012.

A Photographic Gallery

EUGENE REDMOND

...ergo 12 weeks of boot camp
...four weeks of advanced
...ning. They will be eligible
for a 15 day leave after comple-
tion of their training, and they
are to be assigned to a school
or to permanent duty.

(L) Eugene B. Redmond: Lincoln Senior High School, East St. Louis, Illinois. 1957.
(R) EBR: Marine Corps boot camp enlistment announcement. 1958.

EBR: USMC. San Diego, California. 1958.

Program for a reading of Dumas's work. 1975.

Henry Dumas and John Sylvester. Tent City Tenement Development. Setup to protest for housing equality. Leland, Mississippi. 1965.

EBR and Larry Neal at the home of actress and journalist Vertamae Grosvenor. New York City. 1973.

Maya Angelou and EBR. Winston-Salem, North Carolina. 1986.

EBR and siblings. (L-R) Rose Redmond Clark, Lenora Redmond Spencer, Ethel Mae Redmond, EBR, Alma Redmond Foley, John Henry Redmond, Jr., Catherine Redmond Younge. Retirement party for Ethel. Saint Louis, Missouri. 1996.

Members of the EBR Writers Club in East St. Louis. (L-R) EBR, Darlene Roy, Dahveed Nelson (a founding member of the Last Poets), Evon Udoh, Sherman L. Fowler. 1996.

EBR and Treasure Shields Redmond (daughter, 14 years old). 1985.

With lifelong friends. (L-R) Johnny Campbell, Larry Stanberry, EBR, Freddie Murdock (uncle of Olympian Jackie Joyner-Kersee), Roosevelt Peabody.

EBR with former student, Avery Brooks. National Black Arts Festival. Atlanta, Georgia. 1990.

"Da-Dum-Dun"
A Black Arts Movement Triumvirate of Conch/Us/Nest:
Miles Davis, Henry Dumas & Katherine Dunham
in East St. Louis, Illinois

I
Surroundsounddrums
We learned by leading
Surroundsoundmusic
Led by learning
Surroundsoundpoetry
Led & Learned by Yearning
Surroundviewblackness

Spinning & spun by webs of conch-us-nests, hugely & brightly & bluesaically loded with Arkansippi consciousness, upriver driving wheels choo-chooing & checking in at points along 'Sippi's Corridor. Arrivants & dispersants: Until within the nearly limitless number of concentric circles of art & activism in Metro-East St. Louis (Illinois) *cum* Midwest, Miles Dewey Davis III came to occupy the center ring of the dawn, peak & afterglow of the Black Arts & Black Power Movements. Yes, we established common cause & comradeship with other regional centers & stars—Chicago, Detroit, Gary, Indianapolis, Kansas City, Omaha, Minneapolis-St. Paul—but Davis' expressivity, visibility, audibility & (self-styled) breeding/breathless originality, dominated & led other enveloping rings in East Saint's Soular System. To wit, the briefly lit Henry Lee Dumas (HD, Hank) (1934–1968), writer & poet who came to us via Sweet Home (Arkansas), Harlem, the Arabian Peninsula, Texas, Rutgers U. & Hiram College; & Katherine Dunham (KD) (1909–2006), who had spent 30 years in 60 countries—as a dancer, choreographer, activist, anthropologist, filmmaker, author & educator—when she landed here to found the Performing Arts Training Center (PATC), followed in the 1970s & 1980s by her namesake Dynamic Museum & Children's Workshop. Arriving in 1967, both Hank & KD taught at Southern Illinois University's Experiment in Higher Education (EHE), a local star in the national constellation of the Great Society's War on Poverty—& the umbrella for PATC, Upward Bound & other critical new planets in the Soular System. Saxophonist Julius Hemphill of St. Louis's Black Artists' Group (BAG). Painter & Pan African Theorist Oliver Jackson, later of Oberlin College & California State University-Sacramento. Sociologist Joyce Ladner, later of the Institute of the Black World, Hunter College & Howard U. Author Shelby Steele, later of California State University-San Jose. Fiction Writer Jerry Herman of American Friends Service & a Traverser of Africa. All taught at EHE where poet & Dumas protégé Sherman Fowler (then/later of *Negro Digest/Sides of the River/Black American Literature Forum & Drumvoices Revue*), actor Ron Tibbs (later with Danny Glover of San Francisco's American Conservatory Theater's Black Actors Workshop) & filmmaker Warrington Hudlin III (*House Party*/Black Filmmaker Foundation) were students.

An inventory of circles of influence—& how they rippled & resonated across neo- & sub-centers of the Black Arts Movement (BAM)—would require reams of paper & several semesters because the interconnecting & interdisciplinary struggles in East St. Love, like those elsewhere, included native & imported artists, activists & institutions. East Saint felt the direct & vicarious presences/influences of local, national & Third World artists, warriors & warrior-artists like "Leaping" Leon Thomas, Angela Davis, Motown's posse, Malcolm X, Black Panthers, Frantz Fanon, James Brown, John Coltrane, Che Guevara, Stokely Carmichael & H. Rap Brown (the latter two frequent visitors to Arkansippi), Leroi Jones/Amiri Baraka (Lincoln Park circa 1969 w/Simbas) & Sister Sonia, as in Sanchez (who would accompany homeboy Leon on a voyage home in 1972), Fidel Castro—& Cuba!, Kwame Nkrumah, Sekou Toure & Mao Tse Tung. Malcolm X's autobiography & "red book" were among favorite texts.

Miles was a luminous Third Whirl soldier, too, but he was also *ours*: Native Prince, Star (who'd gigged with marquee names: think Bird, Billy, Billie, Monk, Dizzy), Rebel & Paragon in the ozone of jazz. Blowin' through town in the 60's/70's with wife Frances Taylor, former Dunham Company dancer. And later with actress Cicely Tyson ('82) for the naming of Miles Dewey Davis III Elementary School ("Home of the Blue Notes[!]"). Concurrently, we empathized with his wars, scars, phases, cycles, shifts & permutations. Wore tikis & gris gris fashioned from *Kind of Blue's* "All Blues," "Blue and Green," "So What" & "Flamenco Sketches." Adorned ourselves in 1960's jewels like *ESP, Miles Smiles, Sorcerer, Nefertiti, Miles in the Sky, Filles de Kilimanjaro* & the uneclipseable *Bitches Brew.* Devoured & aped (his favorite) writers James Baldwin & Marc Crawford. Then, criss-crossed the US—NYC to East Boogie to Los Angeles—with him. Even 1974's *On the Corner*—with its so-real/surreal cover drawings—conjured up real life corners in the city of homeboy's upbringing. 15th Street at Broadway (site of the 1967 Rebellion where, earlier, Dr. Miles Dewey Davis Sr. planted his dental office & domicile). 15th at Bond Avenue where Miles & siblings attended John Robinson Elementary School (namesake of city's Black patriarch, where Nat Turner's granddaughters—Lucy & Fannie—taught) & St. Paul Baptist Church (where Fannie was organist). 15th at Piggott Avenue where he saw movies at the Lincoln Theater & hung out in Lincoln Park. These features completed the socialization arena that Dumas—in *Jonoah and the Green Stone* (1976)—would refer to as the three-ring concentric circles of home, church & school.

II
The great god Shango in the African Sea
reached down with palm oil and oozed out me.
—HD (in Knees of a Natural Man)

When Henry Lee Dumas & East St. Louis interpenetrated presences in 1967—an act reminiscent of Conrad Kent Rivers' lines, "Wandering through . . . France/As France wandered through me"—it was a rare moment in the Soular System. It was also the final such mutual immersion for Dumas after his birth & early childhood in Sweet Home, Arkansas, and additional youth years in Harlem, New York, before flirting with college, joining the Air Force, marrying & fathering two sons, returning to college & working briefly at Hiram College's

Upward Bound Program in Ohio. African- & bible-centered, musicographic & choreographic, Hank's Sun Ra-inspired planet had already witnessed a succession of self-inventions at a time when the term "identity" was exhaled as naturally as air—& almost as frequently. Nearly 40 years later, in a kwansaba titled "Dumas's Rebirth in Word-Deed," I catalogued some of his favorite personal & family re-inventions during the Black Arts Movement:

> Awake as a quake, dreamin' Henry wrought
> Hank into "Ankh," Dumas into "Samud": named
> his poems "sabas" & "ikefs," his friends
> "Headeye" & "Jonoah," his settings "Sweetwater" &
> "Harlem," his vessels "afro-horn" & "soul-
> boat," his heroes "Probe" & "Sun Ra"
> & his brothers "Fon" & "cosmic arrows."

In Sweet Home, Harlem & elsewhere, Hank became a culturally "stored" & multi-storied boy-man who bonded richly with "villagers," something he accomplished almost instantly with EHE colleagues & students. (You did that during Civil Rights & BAM despite the omnipresent paranoia—we called it "healthy" paranoia—stoked in part by the infiltration of agent provocateurs.) Hank's homework on East St. Louis yielded the city's backdrop via the Great Migration—& 1917 Race Riot; it's nurturing of Miles Davis, Ike & Tina Turner (at the Manhattan Club), Chuck Berry (at the Cosmo Club), Barbara Ann Teer & Leon Thomas (at Lincoln High School, also Miles' alma mater); it's hosting of Katherine Dunham, his new colleague; & its front-drop of poverty, gangs, high unemployment & other hand-me-downs from slavery, Jim Crow & Midwestern apartheid. Riffin' in poems like "East Saint Hell" & "Our King is Dead" (an elegy for MLK), he merged BAM themes—"healthy" paranoia, the scourge of racism, art as self-defense, nationalism & songification of struggle—with localized/East Boogie history & causes. Meanwhile, our self-studies of Hank included imbibing litmags in which he appeared—*Umbra, Hiram Poetry Review Negro Digest* & numerous handouts—along with his infectious love for knowledge, especially Black folklore & music.

Students & faculty—of EHE & PATC—represented a range of socioeconomic & ideological derivations & conditions. But nationalism, thanks to Black Arts/Black Power & Elijah's "Nation," took deepest hold. We slept with one eye open but Hank slept fully awake, as noted by all who knew him, including friend/poet Jay Wright & Loretta Dumas—HD's wife. (At Dumas's funeral in May 1968, a childhood friend said, "Henry thought too deep for the average person.") In December of 1967— in a mixture of real & surreal, mystical & mythical, cosmic & funkadelic—Hank described himself:

> Even the dust of the earth and the gravel and the
> twigs like fingers grappling, even the shadows, even
> these sleepy children of the sun yonder, even the
> family of trees, all these watch me run, hear my passage,
> see me, my phantom style racing across their vision,
> pulsing through their dialogues, and they rejoice,
> and they turn over inside themselves and they say,
> There he goes and there he goes. Look at him.

Attesting to the fecundity & productivity that paralleled such speed are numerous posthumously published collections of his writing from *Poetry for My People* to *Ark of Bones* to *Jonoah and the Green Stone* to *Knees of a Natural Man* to *Echo Tree*. Nobel Laureate Toni Morrison who, along with Amiri Baraka, has been a primary director of the Dumas "cult" cum "movement," called HD "A genius, an absolute genius," who was also "magnetic."

III

> *"Taylor Jones said, 'When I die*
> *I don't want my brothers to cry.*
> *When I go out old death to meet,*
> *I want fire and dancing in the street!'"*

BAM! Words, interwoven with dance, music, song, drums, lights & sets, ushered from the creative genius of Katherine Dunham, exploding on local & national stages less than a year after her arrival in East St. Louis. The words were part of an "ode" inspired by the death of Taylor Jones III, activist & leader of the Midwestern Region of the Congress of Racial Equality (CORE). Dunham's mettle had already been tested a few days after East Boogie's July '67 Rebellion, when she was arrested after going to the aid of a young Black Power spokesman on one of the city's war-torn corners. The Rebellion & Jones' death/funeral fueled the writing & staging of "The Ode to Taylor Jones III."

Beginning with the "Ode," Dunham inserted EHE students, local organizers, activists & orators into skits, ballets, or full-length plays; wrote playlets around specific issues & causes; & incorporated works & words of East St. Louis artists/writers into PATC's fluid & flexible stage events. PATC's recruitment, curriculum & programmatic schedules included bringing the most influential organizers & gang leaders into consciousness & using them to attract theater, drum & dance initiates, many of whom at first sneered at the idea of men dancing on stage & disparaged leotards as "pantyhose." Charles "Swede" Jeffries' Imperial War Lords, Frank Smith's Black Egyptians, Charles Koen's Black Liberators & Lucious Jones' IMPACT House were among gangs &/or organizations that Dunham & EHE helped politicize, enlist in new ideological-intellectual armies of activism, & place on stages of education & cultural arts. Hyman Frankel, Donald Henderson & Edward Crosby, EHE's triumvirate of brilliant leaders, frequently conferenced with Dunham & "street" leaders—resulting in a powerful three-way collaboration of EHE, PATC & residential communities.

Meanwhile, international artists, scholars, activists—including South Africans in exile—statespeople & revolution-aries streamed through our offices, classrooms & workshops. Visitors/consultants included Harry Belafonte & wife Julie, a former Dunham Company member; Eartha Kitt, also a former Company member; Oscar Brown Jr.; D.C. architect Topper Carew; psychologist Erich Fromm (whom we visited in the

Apple, thanks to KD); Mille. Suzanne Diop of the Senegalese Supreme Court; renaissance man R. Buckminster Fuller; Nina Simone; Rap Brown & Stokley Carmichael; Gordon Parks & artist Charles White (from Dunham's Chicago days of leading a Works Project Administration (WPA) writers unit); drummers René Calvin (Haitian) & Mor Thiam (Senegalese); St. Clair Drake; Hattie McDaniel & Brock Peters; & numerous other former Dunham Company members like Lucille Ellis & Tommy Gomez, based upstate in Chicago.

Performing, work-shopping & lecturing throughout metropolitan East St. Louis, members of PATC & EHE also did tours of the Midwest, US & world; hosted student-faculty exchange programs with Nigeria, France & Haiti; & gave classes, workshops & forums in schools, prisons, neighborhood centers, churches bars & restaurants. All of these offerings were, for the most part, extracurricular. But there were of course the main courses: While EHE restructured & renamed those in the General Education curriculum (for example, Joyce Ladner & I co-taught "Socialization of the Black Child," which qualified as "Introduction to Sociology" on the main/Edwardsville campus of SIU), PATC reprised the curriculum of the Dunham School of Dance from 1940's New York. Course offerings, beyond the obvious ones in drumming, dance & acting, included French, Wolof & Haitian Creole languages; African-Diaspora History; textiles, weaving, cooking & sewing; martial arts, including capoeira; poetry & playwriting. From enrollees, Dunham drew members of her newly developing indigenous company. When combined, EHE, PATC & St. Louis organizations like BAG helped form the nation's most comprehensive/inclusive Black Arts Collective during the BAM era. "We must create a theater-going audience," KD said time & time again: "We have to have cultural, literary, consciousness-raising, activist-oriented & performing arts—& audiences for them!" And there was no doubt that Miles "So What" Davis & Henry "Ankh" Dumas were in soul-sync with her.

Riffing Between Rifts: BAG's Grooves

(from Preface to Ben Looker's BAG: "Point from which creation begins")

Thanks to Benjamin Looker's careful and empathetic study, the geographical, political, cultural, racial and artistic territory in which St. Louis's Black Artists' Group (BAG) came into self-awareness and formation will be re-etched (like familiar scarifications) into the memory of those who were there in the fire and ferment of the 1960s and 1970s. The fabled, multi-tiered, and therapeutic stresses of those spatial and temporal terrains—exploding and imploding in regional, national, and worldwide bellies—also resulted in permanent acoustical and optical scarifications. Their legacies, which now reside in the purview of both "orature" and formal pedagogy, have become a natural part of the artistic, investigative, pioneering, and activist spirit that was passed like a baton among descendants, heirs, and beneficiaries of BAG and the Black Arts/Black Power Movements. BAG's trailblazing achievements include being centrally responsible for the creation of a regional Black Arts Movement (BAM); making what Miles Davis called "that St. Louis [art] thing" accessible to the world in both traditional and radicalized forms; establishing beachheads in Europe (including Sweden and France) and Africa; making influential sound waves among musical innovators and audiences in New York's "loft movement"; and extending the St Louis "thing" across the globe by founding the World Saxophone Quarter.

St. Louis's and East St. Louis's historic role in developing and fostering the twin roots of African American racial-social consciousness and musical-literary arts is cogently framed by the strategic geographical-industrial position of these two cities. Both served as winnowing and threshing floors for strategists aiming to advance the cause of black freedom and equality and to eliminate the viruses of racism (recall the Dred Scott Decision in St. Louis and the 1917 race riots in East St. Louis). Both cities also acted as conduits (via railways, packinghouses, and waterways) for the upriver migration of blues, jazz, and gospel from New Orleans, various points of departure in Mississippi, and Memphis. Each was a nurturing and processing ground for musical culture, feeding it to other midwestern locations such as Kansas City and Chicago, as well as East Coast cities such as Philadelphia and New York. Looker richly sums up this influential metroplex by referring to St. Louis as a "hing" city, "fixed geographically and musically midway between Chicago and New Orleans."

Under Looker's "def licks," BAG's portraiture emerges as a multiarts and activist confluence grooving on vibrant tributaries of events, individuals, and organizations, including the densely layered socialization rituals that BAG members experienced while growing up in the Ville or attending St. Louis's segregated public schools (Sumner High in particular) and the historically black Lincoln University in Jefferson City, Missouri. Other tributaries ranged from musicians and mentors such as Clark Terry, Elwood Buchanan, Miles Davis, George Hudson, Eddie Randall, Chuck Berry, Ken Billups, Ike Turner, and Freddie Washington to Pulitzer Prize-winning poet Gwendolyn Brooks and French playwright Jean Genet (whose work *The Blacks* served as BAG's inaugural arts event). Nor does Looker overlook BAG's enormous debt to dancer-choreographer Katherine Dunham's Performing Arts Training Center (PATC) or to John Coltrane, Ornette Coleman, Albert Ayler, Archie Shepp, and Chicago's Association for the Advancement of Creative Musicians (AACM). Aware that they were part of a larger national and global cultural ambience, BAG participants pioneered the ideal—a "holistic" (if that's the right word) multi-arts commune often touted but never fully realized by other BAM collectives.

In particular, BAG's holism was aided in its conceptualization, implementation, and empowerment by Dunham's PATC and Southern Illinois University's Experiment in Higher Education (EHE). Located in East St. Louis, the EHE, which housed PATC, was a veritable fulcrum of art, radical curriculum development (especially emerging black studies programs), pan-Africanism (and other cutting-edge ideologies), activism, and leadership training for the "movement." The mere presence of the legendary Katherine Dunham—not to mention the radicalized and unorthodox faculties and student bodies of

EHE and PATC—augured well for the various social, political, and aesthetic thrusts in the St. Louis metroplex and urban America at large. Complementing Dunham's presence and importance was that of St. Louis painter-thinker Oliver Jackson, whose portrait is also deftly etched by Looker. Jackson, an unheralded but brilliant architect of pan-African concepts, aesthetics, and curricula, was also chief theoretician at the EHE-PATC complex and helped usher in black studies programs at Southern Illinois University-Edwardsville, Oberlin College, Ohio University, and California State University-Sacramento, where he laid the theoretical groundwork for a pan-African studies department that still thrives.

Jackson conceived and put into the place the sets and images for Images: Sons/Ancestors, an ambitious and hugely successful mixed-media performance of the African Continuum (Jackson's favorite phrase) at St. Louis's Powell Symphony Hall in February of 1971. (Jackson also took the continuum concept to CSU-Sacramento where, working with dramaturge Paul Carter Harrison, he gave the name Sons/Ancestors to CSU's award-winning African American theater program.) The African continuum program showcased BAG members (and associates such as pianist John Hicks and Senegalese master drummer Mor Thiam) at the peak of their powers—and in one of the city's literal and symbolic citadels of European-Anglo-American art and culture. "Images," a variant of which BAG would produce repeatedly throughout the bistate region, meshed "high" black art with symbols and repositories of "high" white art and told volumes about the backgrounds of BAG members and allies, including their intensive cross-cultural and cross-fertilized aesthetics and training. Such "crosses" included the aforementioned upbringing and chops-cutting, explorations of African art and thought (thanks to Jackson's prodding), and the impact of and/or collaborations with European classical-modernist-radical composers such as John Cage, Arthur Custer, and Karlheinz Stockhausen. Underlying all of these confluent energies were the magnetic, diverse, and painful origins of St. Louis, from the ever-green burial sites of the Osage and Underground Railroad hideaways to Pierre Laclède's dominions and Scott Joplin's "rags" to W.C. Handy's blues and the East St. Louis race riots (which inspired the formation of the St. Louis Urban League in 1918).

BAG was not, by any stretch of the imagination, the best-known BAM collective—that distinction, as Looker duly notes, belonged to such groups as LeRoi Jones's (Amiri Baraka's) New York Black Arts Repertory Theatre and School (and Spirit House in Newark), Oakland's Black House, Chicago's Organization of Black American Culture (OBAC), and Los Angeles's Watts Writers Workshop. However, St. Louis had ties to more popular and influential BAM units: BAG poet Bruce (Ajulé) Rutlin attended workshops at Gwen Brooks's home in Chicago, for example, and St. Louis native Quincy Troupe, a member of the Watts Workshop, maintained ties with BAG members, some of whom he had known since high school. Troupe helped link BAG and East and West Coast BAM artists and activists through associations with Baraka, Sun Ra, Ornette Coleman, Larry Neal, Jayne Cortez, K. Curtis Lyle, Stanley Crouch, and others.

Under the leadership of Julius Hemphill, the brilliant jazz-voiced Rutlin, poet-composer Oliver Lake, baritonist Hamiet Bluiett, and the restlessly inventive Lester Bowie, BAG stretched out, simultaneously embracing and developing what East St. Louis jazz deejay Leo Chears called "different bags." BAG's "bags" included poetry (a.k.a. the spoken arts) with Robert Malinké Elliott, Shirley Bradley LeFlore (then wife of BAG trumpeter Floyd LeFlore), and, later, highly original Watts Workshop transplant K. Curtis Lyle. The dance and theater components flourished under the leadership of Georgia Collins (borrowed from Dunham's PATC), Portia Hunt, Muthal Naidoo, and the idiosyncratic and brilliant Vincent Terrell. Visual artists Emilio Cruz (visiting from New York) and Oliver Jackson vigorously engaged their respective interests as BAG launched mixed forms that encompassed everything from "guerilla" theater to all-night sidewalk jam sessions.

Looker's examination of the impact of racial dynamics on BAG and black music and musicians nationwide is particularly telling as he surveys the demographics and economics of race, black migration, and audiences. Social and economic gains and setbacks created by the northern migration of blacks were mirrored by the success and plummeting fortunes of the musicians. The burgeoning new black middle class initially aided in the flourishing of jazz clubs and buying market for recorded jazz, but new patterns of segregation—supported by entrenched St. Louis racism—kept black musicians from playing in white venues even as the black sources of support for jazz dried up. The downturn in support came courtesy of the open (and ambivalent) arms of suburbia. Looker spends well-directed energy on the phenomenon, including the role of big, small, and self-operated recording companies. Fore example, we are told that in 1972 no less a genius than Julius Hemphill sat in his LaClede Town home, hand-labeling copies of his inaugural and seminal recording, *Dogon A.D.*, for distribution to radio stations, jazz magazines, and music critics.

Looker's rich reportage and evaluative writing highlights the sticky issue of black artist-audience interactions and protocol—a particularly complex and often avoided subject but one that is always circulating on the grapevine. With BAG, artist-audience communication (or lack thereof) was paramount because of the collective's new and radically out-there "bag," in the face of an already diminishing audience in an already conservative "belt" (and already in a former slave state). Alternatively heartbroken from playing to near-empty houses and exhilarated by standing-room-only audiences, BAG also underwent merciless and unabashedly negative criticism from elder statesmen and peers married to conventional and "acceptable" ways of performing music, poetry, theater, and dance. In one of the most judicious and courageous discussions in print, Looker examines all sides of this issue—economic, social, racial, geographical, class, gender, and taste. Noting that perceptions are central to the issue of artist-audience relationships, he discusses stereotypes that each side holds of the other. Should an audience have to snap fingers, shake booties, and/or pat feet? Can they just sit and listen?

Down on the threshing floor of aesthetics, ideologies, perceptions, issues, and managing and playing a day-to-day schedule, BAG continued its dynamic program of "musical institution-building," employing three primary initiatives:

> First, and most crucially, BAG's artist resituated ... and redefined the traditional spaces for jazz performance. In discarding the customary club gigs . . . they eluded aesthetic restrictions and cultivated an inner-city listenership whose ears would otherwise have remained deaf to their brand of music. Second, by initiating reciprocal activities with other like-minded collective[s] . . . they helped to create a broad, supportive network of experimental musicians throughout the Midwest. And, finally, by starting their own record labels [Mbari, Universal Justice] ... several of BAG's musicians tried to create an alternative cultural space for their music, one in which they could at least partly escape the commercial pressures threatening to squeeze the life out of the music.

Among the aforementioned experimental Midwest collectives with which BAG interacted were Katherine Dunham's Performing Arts Training Center (where Hemphill taught) and Black River Writers Press in East St. Louis; Mor Thiam's Senegalese-spiced drum and dance ensemble; AACM of Chicago; St. Louis/East St. Louis institutions and venues such as Gateway Theatre, Circle Coffee Shop and Bookstore, Berea Presbyterian Church, IMPACT House, Webster College, Sheldon Memorial Hall, City Art Museum in Forest Park; and Detroit's Creative Musicians Association, John Sinclair's Artists Workshop, and Phil Raelin and Wendell Harrison's Tribe. However, these connections, vibrant as they were, could not compete with the changes and challenges generally experience by jazz musicians and BAG's free-avant-experimental grooves in particular.

Reasons for BAG's breakup and death—in its St. Louis matrix—have been attributed to numerous differences and tensions, from economic and administrative to artistic and ideological to personal and aesthetic. According to Hemphill, BAG, which hadn't "cultivated" younger cadres of artists, lacked the material and emotional support to stay alive. The drying-up of audience support was also a factor, as noted by BAG members and friends. BAG remained in the African American "grain," however; according to Looker, when five of its members headed to Paris in 1972, they "replicated the transatlantic journey of half a century's worth of African American musicians, visual artists, and writers." However, in Paris, Sweden, and elsewhere in Europe, the economic and attitudinal ups and downturns took heavy tolls on the artists as they had in St. Louis, and BAG members headed for New York and the "loft scene," where colleague Hamiet Bluiett (who had earlier opted not to go to Paris) had established a foothold.

In New York, BAG again "grooved" on the winnowing and threshing floor of aesthetics and entrepreneurship and returned to the gig life in 1976, riffing out of its reincarnated "bag" as the World Saxophone Quartet. The rest, as they croon, rests with "bags" of stories about BAG's grooves.

Yes, BAG folded—but its folding, as that of other Black Arts Movement collectives across the country, did not signal the collapse of the numerous spin-off "BAGs." Just check out a sample listing of the contemporary bistate heirs to BAG's legacy: writers Arthur Brown, Chris Mullen, Jabari Asim, Andrea Wren, Sylvester Brown, Ruth Miriam Garnett, Chris Hayden, Sherman L. Folwer, and Darlene Roy (and members of the eighteen-year-old Eugene B. Redmond Writers Club in East St. Louis); participants in the highly visible and audible spoken arts movement; musicians Glenn Papa Wright, Reginald Thomas, Montez Coleman, Russell Gunn, Delano Redmond, and Keyon Harold; dance/drum ensembles such as the Bakari Institute, Sylvester "Sunshine" Lee's Community Performance Ensemble, Deborah Ahmed and Black Dance St. Louis, and the East St. Louis Center for the Performing Arts; and acting ensembles such as St. Louis Black Repertory, Unity Theater, and Pamoja

Theater. Even more popular and commercially successful artists and entertainers like Cedric, Nelly, Chingy, and the Hudlin Brothers' filmmaking team can trace their origins back to BAG— not to mention TV producer and St. Louis fiction sensation Lyah LeFlore, daughter of BAG artist Floyd LeFlore and Shirley Bradley Leflore.

Benjamin Looker has set a pace and a standard for "bagging" the grooves of modern and contemporary Black Arts movements in a cultural, racial, artistic, and economic context. Now the work of biographers, autobiographers, ethnologists, musicologists, sociologists, cultural workers, and philosophers— coming out of the new, newer and newest "BAGs"—must begin.

A Blues Taps for Harold Washington
1922–1987

A bonafide black American folk hero, Chicago Mayor Harold Washington, is dead at the age of 65—a victim of over-weening love for, and commitment to, his people and humankind. Like the late Clyde C. Jordan (1930–1987), Mr. Washington gave and planned and conferenced, and then repeated the same process many times, until he could give no more. Because of who he was, what he stood for, and the far-reaching dimension of his dream-work, Harold Washington's death creates a tidal wave of grief in his Windy City home and across the Black Diaspora. More than the emotional pain-loss caused by Mr. Washington's departure, though, is the vast canyon-like vacancy left within the ranks of Chicago's leadership. By paying studious attention to his legacy, however, survivors can move with dispatch to calm political storms and build upon the rich "movement" he began.

There were many levels and sides to the articulate, brilliant, art-inspired, folk-based, dynamic, peripatetic and dream-weaving Mr. Washington (making attempts to replace him all the more difficult). Wherever he went, whatever he did, or however he was confronted, he was predictably a man-for-all-seasons in his manner, his response and his wise approach to leadership. The tragedy is that this strong, forthright, proud pioneer of Chicago and Black-World Political Change, was snatched from his pilot's seat on the dawn of his Big Dream. This is not to say, however, that other dreams—of varying magnitudes—weren't his to know before his death. For he had inextricably linked Chicago to the New World Revolution in ethnicity, culture, economics, art, politics and race. But the larger dream, that of consolidating all of his life's efforts under one wonderful roof of cross-cultural continuity, had not been brought to full fruition.

Nevertheless, Harold Washington will be long remembered, and emulated, for his tough-sweet application of ancestral folkways as he sparred eloquently with bigots, high-handed do-gooders, walking deadheads and doomsayers. Though this magnificent statesman-hero's death has temporarily plunged his native Chicago and the Black World into confusion and grief, the "movement" of which he so fondly spoke will carry his legendary beacon on to the next curve in the struggle, to the next intersection in the people's spiraling trail onward and upward.

In October of 1986, at a church on Chicago's Southside, Mayor Harold Washington said: "We have elevated struggle to the level of fine art." No one, in recent memory, contributed more to that elevation than Harold Washington himself.

Reprinted from the *East St. Louis Monitor*, 1987

Cataloging Toward an
Autobiography of an Archive
November 2011, East St. Harlem

41 years ago September last
(i.e. 8 months before the birth of my youngest daughter
Treasure Shields Redmond,
1 month after Quincy Troupe & I met in St. Louis
enroute to Ohio as writers-in-residence: he @ O.U.
& I @ Oberlin where I'd meet Russell Atkins, Norman
Jordan & Karamu House in nearby Cleveland—

      & Calvin Hernton who succeeded me @ Oberlin,

13 months after the death of my Beloved Grandmother
Rosa A. Quinn,
22 years following the passing of my Mother Emma Jean
Hutchinson Redmond
& 5 years before my Father John Henry Redmond Sr. slipped
into Ancestorhood,
19 years after being devirginized by a friend's aunt who'd been
widowed by the Korean Conflict);

41 years ago September last
(i.e. 3 years & 3 months after I became bodyguard,
chauffeur, confidant &
    translator to Katherine Dunham @ her Performing Arts
    Training Center & a colleague of Henry Lee Dumas, Oliver
    Jackson & Joyce Ladner @ Southern Illinois University's
    Experiment in Higher Education in East St. Louis,

1 month after (again) leaving East Saint Arkansippi to join
English, Ethnic & Pan African
    Studies Departments @ California State University
    Sacramento,
6 years before being named Poet Laureate of East St. Louis;
yes, 41 years ago . . .
11 months after meeting Robert Hayden, Steve Cannon,
Stanley Crouch, Ishmael Reed &
    Maurice Lubin at a '69 Inter-American Writers Congress

in Buffalo (New York),
4 months after publication of my first slim volume of verse,
Sentry of the Four Golden Pillars, by Black River Writers Press,
6 years before Doubleday's release of my critical history,
Drumvoices: The Mission of Afro-American Poetry, & 20 years
        before the founding of *Drumvoices Revue: A Confluence
        of Literary/Cultural/Vision Arts*,
18 years before my first trip to Africa where I
photographed & interviewed Fela Anikalapo Kuti
wearing fashion underwear & 14 wives);

41 years ago September last
(i.e. 9 years after leaving Southeast Asia, courtesy of
the US Marines, & returning
        to college & Midwest Street Heat,
3 years after hosting H. Rap Brown & Stokely
Carmichael amidst East Boogie's
        Black Rebellion—50 years following the 1917
        Riot that inspired a silent mournful march of
        thousands in New York City,
6 & 7 years respectively after winning a Pushcart Prize
& a National Endowment
        for the Arts Creative Writing Fellowship,
2 years after becoming Dumas's literary executor, with
the blessings of his widow
        Loretta & in collaboration with Amiri Baraka &
Toni Morrison,
2 years/4 months after MLK's assassination & 5
years/4months after Malcolm's
        who, Hayden said, "x'd his name" into our
conch-us-nest);

41 years ago September last
(i.e.16 years before the now 25-year-old EBR Writers Club—
placed in the Trusteeship of Margaret Walker Alexander,
Maya Angelou, Amiri, Avery Brooks, Gwendolyn Brooks,
Raymond Patterson, Barbara Ann Teer, Quincy, Jerry Ward
& Lena Weathers (a posse of literati later joined by Haki R.

Madhubuti)—was chartered by Sherman Fowler, Darlene Roy
& EBR . . .);

41 years ago September last,
Maya & I, who'd glimpsed each other @ sundry gatherings
for the good, met fast & formally @ Sacramento City College,
where a hipper than hip student body had voted Angela
Yvonne Davis in as Homecoming Queen, & where, riffin'
poetically, Maya—my new Sister—said, "Eugene, be my
Brother forever!"

CPSIA information can be obtained at www.ICGtesting.com
Printed in the USA
BVOW07s1759280714

360618BV00002B/2/P